The Apocalypse in Rudolf Steiner's Lecture Series

The Apocalypse in Rudolf Steiner's Lecture Series

Charles Kovacs

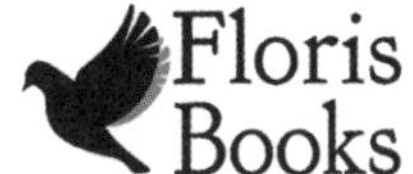

First published in 2013 by Floris Books
Second printing 2021

British Library CIP Data available
ISBN 978-178250-014-8
Printed and bound in Great Britain by Bell & Bain, Ltd

 Floris Books supports sustainable forest management
by printing this book on materials made from wood that
comes from responsible sources and reclaimed material

Contents

Foreword

Charles Kovacs was for many years a class teacher at the Edinburgh Rudolf Steiner School. Many of his notes on various main lesson subjects have already been published in Floris Books and are now well known in educational circles. Less well known, however, is the fact that over four decades he regularly led anthroposophical study groups at different locations in Edinburgh. These were attended by a variety of people from the anthroposophical community in and beyond the city.

The present volume contains his own preparatory notes for a series of fourteen such meetings based on Rudolf Steiner's Apocalypse lectures, though, as always, he never used the notes during the meetings. Although accessible to any interested reader, the study left to us by Mr Kovacs comes from a deep knowledge of anthroposophy and links to many contemporary questions.

Included are also sketches of the seven seals of the Apocalypse which Clara Rettich made following Rudolf Steiner's indications. They werer created for decorating the hall in Munich where the Theosophical Congress of 1907 was to take place.

Throughout his life Mr Kovacs was also a talented artist and a small selection of his paintings has been included in this book. These pictures have been chosen to relate to the themes in the lectures but were not originally painted to accompany any text.

Some people may be aware that a similar volume by Charles Kovacs was published in German in 2011 by Perseus Verlag entitled *Betrachtung zur Apokalypse*. The two books have broadly the same content but differ in detail. Neither is a translation; each was given originally in its own language to different groups of people.

1

The Lord of Time

Rudolf Steiner's cycle of lectures on the Apocalypse comprises twelve lectures preceded by an introduction. On first reading, the introduction may seem no more than a formal welcome, but mere formality is not Rudolf Steiner's style and what he said on this occasion is of significance for the whole cycle. With the insight of the present day we may even discern a meaning in the fact that the lectures were given in Nuremberg, the site of the Nuremberg trials which led to the execution of Hitler's accomplices for crimes against humanity; crimes which, for their scale and brutality, should have made mankind aware that we are already entering the era when the beast of the Apocalypse rises from the abyss.

But the real significance of the introductory lecture arises in the personalities mentioned on this occasion. Since Rudolf Steiner refers to Nuremberg, one might have expected that he would mention the most famous son of this ancient city, the painter Albrecht Dürer. He did not do so, but instead spoke of two personalities who, although they lived there for a time, had no real connection with the city or with each other: Hegel and Caspar Hauser. The philosopher Georg Wilhelm Friedrich Hegel was called to Nuremberg not for his abstract, yet profound world conception, but to administer a secondary school. Caspar Hauser stumbled into Nuremberg without knowing where he was or who he was. The temporary sojourn of the two men in Nuremberg would hardly justify their being mentioned in this context. The justification lies in the personalities themselves.

Hegel is known for his philosophy, for the power of his thinking; his personal and private life, although well documented, is of no interest to the world. Caspar Hauser had hardly developed any intellectual abilities at all and his origin was surrounded by mystery. It is his short tragic life that has held and still holds the attention of the world. Hegel is an outstanding representative of thinking, while Caspar Hauser is a living symbol of will. We have to consider that Rudolf Steiner once said about him that after his death he kept humankind connected with the spiritual world at a time (the late nineteenth century) when this connection was in acute danger of being broken.

Thinking, represented by Hegel, reaches from before birth into earth life. Will, represented by Caspar Hauser, reaches from earth life into life after death. Just as a composer introduces a theme in the beginning of a symphony which is later developed and raised to ever greater power, so there sounds in the mentioning of Hegel and Caspar Hauser a theme or motif, whose the polarity recurs again and again in the later lectures.

We shall recognise this polarity again when we come to the two pillars Jachim and Boaz, but we meet it already in the first lecture after the introduction. There Rudolf Steiner describes the difference between the forms of the ancient initiation and the Rosicrucian path. The ancient initiation worked through thinking, the Rosicrucian works through the will. We have therefore the polarity of thought and will in the contrast between ancient and modern initiation.

It is, however, quite a surprise to hear that modern initiation is connected with will if one remembers how often Rudolf Steiner emphasises the importance of thinking. The contradiction is resolved if one realises what Rudolf Steiner means by 'pure thinking' or 'sense-free thinking'. It is in reality sheer will, but applied in a region where it is not normally used at all, in the realm of thought.

The nature of the ancient initiation on the path of thinking follows from the fact that in those times the etheric body was in a much looser connection with the physical body than it is now, and human beings were in consequence less awake than in modern times. In the process of initiation they had to reach, one could say, artificially what modern man has naturally. They had to experience a death process which is the physical basis of our modern consciousness. For modern human beings the task is the reverse. They have to loosen the connection between the etheric and physical bodies, and this is a task of the will. This is also the reason why Rudolf Steiner's books are so 'difficult', for they demand an effort of will in the realm of thinking. If they were 'easy' it would amount to a betrayal of the principles of the Rosicrucian initiation.

We can now ask: who was the first man to go through the new initiation? The answer is that he is also the man who was the last to receive the old initiation. It was the disciple John who, as Lazarus, was initiated by Christ himself. What took place at the tomb in Bethany was at the same time the last old and the first new initiation. At the so-called 'awakening' of Lazarus, Christ stands outside the tomb and calls on Lazarus to come forth. In this act he officiates in the same way as did the hierophant in the ancient mystery ritual. At the same time Lazarus feels in his own being the power to rise from the death-like sleep in which he had lain for three days. He felt the Christ-impulse within himself, which is the principle of the new initiation.

This double nature of the awakening of Lazarus is emphasised by Rudolf Steiner in the book Christianity as Mystical Fact. Lazarus-John, who was initiated by Christ, is not only the writer of the Gospel of St John but also the author of the Apocalypse. It was to him that the future evolution of mankind was revealed on the island of Patmos. His book about the Revelation, or Apocalypse, begins with a vision of a being whose words to him are, 'I am the Alpha and the Omega,' the beginning and the end (Rev.1:8). Greek is the language in which the Apocalypse is written and in the Greek alphabet Alpha (A) is the first letter and Omega (Ω) is the last. However, the real significance of the words spoken by this being lies in the shapes of these two letters, which many people have seen as two of the signs that anthroposophists put on their Christmas trees. The deeper meaning of the Alpha and the Omega, however, is not so widely understood.

In the lectures known as The Study of Man or The Foundations of Human Existence, Rudolf Steiner draws attention to the difference between the bones that form the human head, and those that form the arms and legs. The former are spherical, the latter in comparison are straight. The importance of this lies in the fact that the forces that form the skull are the forces of the limbs of the previous incarnation. The head is, as it were, the end of the forces that come from the past. The forces at present working in the straight limb bones, however, reach into the future. They will form the head of the next incarnation. They are therefore at present still a beginning.

When we now look with this concept in mind at the Greek letters Alpha and Omega, we can recognise in A the image of the limb forces and in Ω the image of the head forces. The site of Christ's crucifixion was called Golgotha, which means 'place of the skull.' It is the place of the end, the Ω to which Christ added the A of the resurrection. Thus the being who speaks to John is not talking of the beginning and end as abstract concepts but as real forces, the forces which link the human being with past and future incarnations, and death with resurrection.

There is still something else to be considered in this context. The forces that are active in forming the head come from the cosmos; the forces that form the limbs come from the earth. The Ω refers to the cosmos, the A to earth. The being who says 'I am the Alpha and the Omega' pronounces with these words that he is the being who unites cosmos and earth – and that means the Christ.

At the time of the ancient mysteries, Christ was a cosmic being in the spiritual world, and so initiation had to seek him on the path of the cosmic force forming the head, on the path of thinking. Since the Mystery of Golgotha, Christ has united himself with the earth and the new initiation has therefore to seek him on the path of will. The Ω initiation of the ancient mysteries, just because it was connected with forces that came from the past, depended upon man's karmic disposition. It was therefore limited to a few individuals. The A initiation depends only upon the human will, irrespective of past karma. It is for all humankind. All this is implied in the simple words 'I am the Alpha and the Omega.'

There is in the Apocalypse also a description of the being who speaks these words. His hair is white like wool but his feet are like burnished bronze, metal molten by fire. What makes our hair white is old age. The white hair is an image for the forces that make us old. As regards the feet, Rudolf Steiner describes the forces working on the child when it begins to walk upright as being like fiery, molten metal. Around the head of this being are the forces of old age, and streaming upwards from the feet are the forces of childhood. Here again is the polarity of head and will, for the head is always old, even when we are young, and the will is always young, even when we are old. But what lies between childhood and old age? The whole of human life. And this life runs its course in a seven-year rhythm. This is the meaning of the seven stars in the hand of this being. But the life of the cosmos also goes through seven stages, from Saturn to the Vulcan stage. This is indicated by the seven candlesticks. As candles illuminate a room, so the seven stages of evolution illuminate and make comprehensible the path mankind has to travel. This is the reason why Rudolf Steiner put so much emphasis on evolution in all his books.

What is then the meaning of the whole picture? It is an image of man as a being of time; beginning and end, youth and old age. The seven-year rhythm and the stages of evolution all refer to time, and human existence in time. Man is not only a spatial being but also a being in time. This is what the vision seen by John wants to convey, and as if to emphasise this true nature of man, the first of the seven seals painted according to Rudolf Steiner's instructions shows the being described in the Apocalypse as walking.

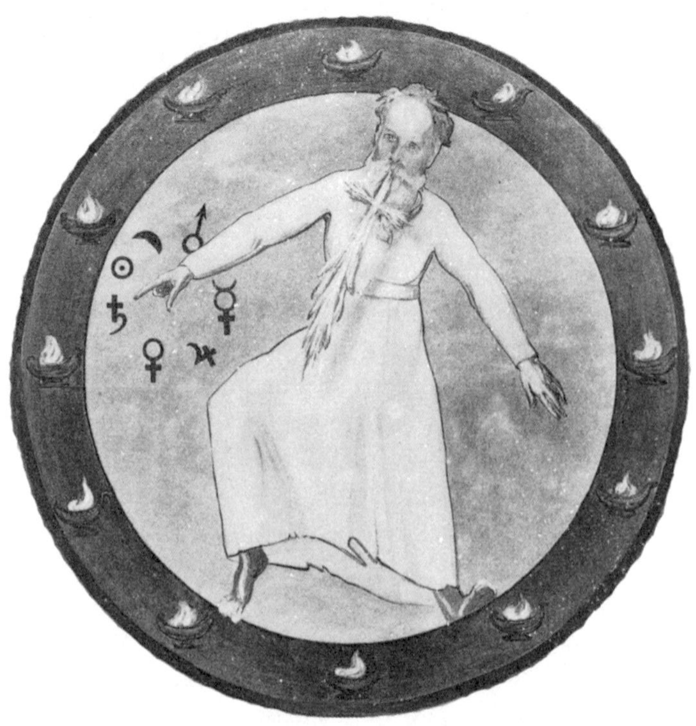

Sketch of the first seal of the Apocalypse

But with this time-element in mind, there arises the possibility of not keeping in step with time. Through this there comes about a division between souls that have developed in tune with time and those who have failed to do so. The symbol of this division is the sword.

Christ is the Lord of Time. He is the power that determines what is the right time for every stage of human development. And so it is his word that, like a sword, divides those who keep pace with the demands of time and those who fail to do so. The Book of Revelation opens with a vision of Christ as Lord of Time and it is he who reveals in the following chapters of the Apocalypse what will be demanded of man by time.

2

The Four Beasts of the Apocalypse

In the first lecture on the Apocalypse Rudolf Steiner speaks about the difference between initiation in ancient times and the modern Rosicrucian path. It is a profound difference, as can be seen by a comparison of the yoga path with modern initiation. All forms of spiritual training, ancient or modern, aim at the development of the chakras or lotus flowers, as they are called. The yoga method, which can be regarded as representative for all ancient systems, begins with the development of the four-petalled chakra that lies in the region of the sex organs. This chakra is activated by the transformation of the sex forces into spiritual forces. This is only possible if one accepts an ascetic, celibate way of life. Then the development of the chakras continues in an upward direction and reaches a very high stage when the chela (disciple) can activate the two-petalled chakra in the middle of the forehead.

The Rosicrucian path begins with the development of the two-petalled chakra. This spiritual organ is the first mentioned in Knowledge of Higher Worlds, but the book contains no instructions about its development. The reason for this seeming omission is that the two-petalled chakra is the organ of 'ego consciousness' or 'consciousness of the self' which is, in fact, quite natural to modern human beings, if they can rid themselves of materialistic prejudices. It is also the organ of 'sense-free' thinking, and this is developed by the proper study of spiritual science. The study itself leads therefore to the activation of this chakra, and no other instructions are needed.

Then the Rosicrucian system proceeds in a downward direction to the chakras in the regions of the larynx, the heart, and so on. This system is therefore not concerned with physical, ascetic practices – it emphasises the need to master one's thoughts, feelings and will impulses. It calls for an inner asceticism of the soul forces which is, if anything, more demanding than the physical abstinence required by the genuine yoga path.

However, in the ancient mystery schools, as in yoga, spiritual development was from the start connected with the transformation of the sex forces and therefore with a celibate life. The sex forces are, from a spiritual aspect, the instrument of the group-souls. They are the means by which certain mental and physical characteristics are transmitted from generation to generation. It is Yahweh who implanted the sex forces into man. The group-souls of the nations and races of the world are his servants. And when in the ancient mystery schools those forces were not used to beget children but were spiritualised, they led the souls capable of such transformation to their particular group-souls. These group-souls belong to the hierarchy of the archangels.

Modern human beings have to find the connection with the archangel of their nation through developing a sense for the specific spiritual quality of their mother language. In ancient times the connection was made by the practices mentioned before.

However, in the second lecture Rudolf Steiner reveals something about the archangels which is not mentioned anywhere else in his work. The group-souls themselves form groups ruled by higher spirits. They are the group-souls of the group-souls. There are four such groups and the powers ruling them are called Lion, Eagle, Bull and Man. In the Apocalypse it is written that these four 'beasts' or 'living creatures' stand before the throne of God (Rev.4:6). This means that they belong to the first hierarchy, who beholds the Father God face-to-face.

The task of these exalted beings is to bring the divine intentions from the timeless, eternal realm of the Father into time. They created the zodiac, which is the expression of the transition from eternity into time. The zodiac is the cosmic 'clock' which shows what is the will of God the Father at any given time. This is the meaning of the clock numerals shown on the surrounding circle of the second seal.

The zodiac is out there in the cosmos but it has a physical counterpart: the human body. Rudolf Steiner confirmed the ancient tradition that links our body with the signs of the zodiac – the head with Aries, the neck with Taurus, etc. And this physical body is the work of the same beings whose cosmic expression is the zodiac: the first hierarchy – or Lion, Eagle, Bull and Man.

When we sleep the I leaves the physical body and these beings enter the body and preserve it. And then, as Rudolf Steiner describes it, the initiate sees the forms of Lion, Eagle, Bull and Man when he regards clairvoyantly the body of a sleeping person.

The form of the human physical body is given to us by inheritance. It is handed down to us by our forebears. It is therefore the work of the group-souls and the group-souls of the group-souls, Lion, Eagle, Bull, Man, which appear to the initiate.

The physical body, this work of the mighty beings of the first hierarchy, is also the most perfect member of the human organisation. It is a 'model' showing how opposing forces can be harmonised. The human soul is still far from achieving such reconciliation of opposites within itself. The resulting disharmony is reflected in the social and political crises of our time. In the lecture cycle, *Man as Symphony*, Rudolf Steiner describes the present situation as arising from a power struggle between the forces of Lion, Eagle and Bull. The Eagle forces are predominant in the West, the Bull forces in the East and the Lion forces in the middle, in Europe. The harmonising principle, Man, is absent. This is the reality behind the tensions and convulsions of the present. The future of human evolution, the coming age of brotherhood, depends on human souls learning to harmonise these contending forces. This ideal has been put in a German fairytale where the symbols are disguised but easily recognisable.

> A cock, a cat, a dog and a donkey had all run away from their owners. Chance brought them together and they decided to form a band of musicians. They came to a forest where they looked for shelter for the night. Eventually they found a house but, looking through the window, they saw that the inhabitants were robbers who would not offer them hospitality. The animals decided to get these evil people out of the house. The dog jumped on the back of the donkey, the cat on the back of the dog and the cock settled on top. They placed themselves in front of the window and began to crow, bark and bray as loudly as they could. When the robbers heard the awful noise and saw the strange monster at the window they thought the devil was after them, ran out of the house and disappeared into the forest. Now the animals could come in and make themselves at home.

In this story the cock, the cat and the donkey are substituted for Eagle, Lion and Bull. The dog, man's best friend, stands for Man. The robbers are our selfish instincts and desires which have to be driven out. The noise that terrifies the robbers is, in reality, the cosmic harmony of the four beasts of the Apocalypse. And the house where they make themselves at home is the human body. The story describes what happens every time we fall asleep.

The physical body of Man is indeed, as we have seen, the 'home' of the four beasts. They are shown in the second seal as the mighty rulers of the human form. In their midst is a lamb, the symbol for the sign Aries, which signifies spring, a new beginning.

The physical body, represented by the four beasts, is the end of an evolution which began on Ancient Saturn. The self that incarnates in this body is the beginning of a new evolution that reaches far into the future. This is meant by the lamb. The secrets of the future are contained in the book on which the lamb lies. However, the self can only fulfil its true destiny through the power of Christ, who is called the Lamb of God. This is what the second seal wants to convey.

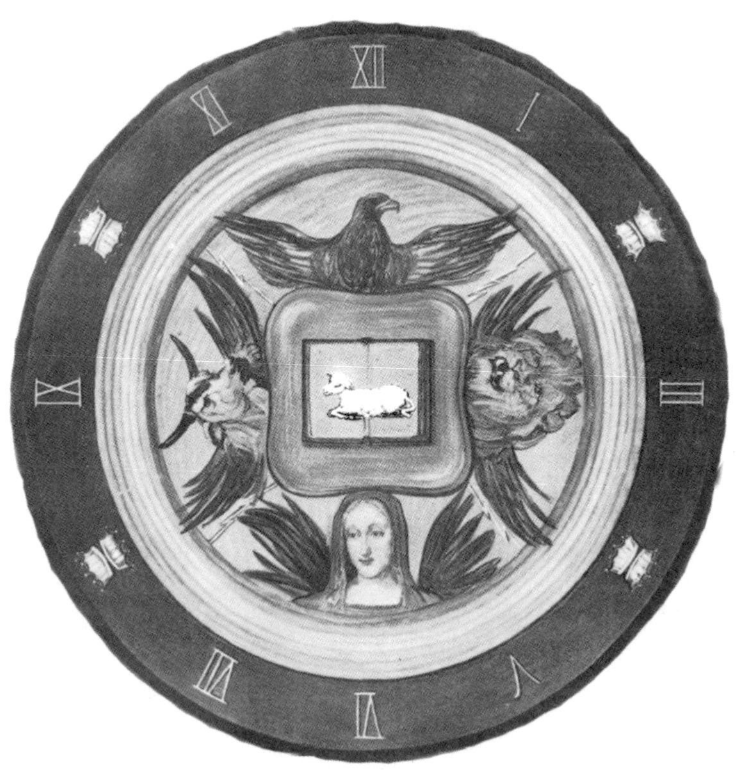

Sketch of the second seal of the Apocalypse

3

The First Four Messages to the Churches

Rudolf Steiner said once, 'Anyone who reads one of my books and is not to some extent changed by it, has not really read it.' He could not mean that one should become noticeably more clever or a better person simply by reading his books – the history of the Anthroposophical Society would be different if it were so. But there is indeed one change which has to take place if one wants to understand even a little of the content of his books – it is a change in our thinking. Certain ideas that one has held without questioning them become problems, riddles, mysteries. Such a concept is 'time'. The lectures about the Apocalypse in particular make it necessary to revise the usual concept of time.

We notice the difference between day and night and the seasonal changes, but otherwise hours, days, months, years, are neutral units without any specific meaning. It does not occur to us that every hour or day or year has a character of its own as if each were a different being. Yet that is what they are, and that is why something that is right today, can be wrong tomorrow or next year. In every moment and on every day and in every epoch there is something which is due, which is new, and which in this particular portion of time is right. These impulses come from eternity into time; so through them the divine intentions are carried into time.

There is also a reverse process. Man lives on earth in time

but the fruits of his deeds in time are carried after death into the realm of eternity. And the being who decides what eternity demands of man, the being who also decides which human achievements are worthy to be carried from time into eternity, this being is Christ. He is the judge of eternity and time. And as this judge he speaks to the post-Atlantean epochs which, in the Apocalypse, are represented by seven churches.

The first judgment or 'message' concerns the church of Ephesus. Rudolf Steiner explained that the people there were in their outlook very similar to the people of the Ancient Indian civilisation, and so Ephesus is a symbol for the first civilisation after the end of Atlantis, the civilisation of Ancient India. It was a civilisation that still felt a strong connection with the spiritual world and did not value earthly existence very highly. Christ's message to the people who have this attitude first praises them for their spiritual striving, but this is then followed by a strange admonition. They are reprimanded for having forgotten their 'first love' (Rev.2:4). These words refer to a great mystery.

It was during the Lemurian period that human souls began to incarnate, but they were not born as souls enter physical bodies now. The earth was of a much finer substance and human beings too were of a different nature. The human etheric body possessed both male and female forces of reproduction. This enabled the soul to form its own physical body directly from the fine earthly matter. So the forces that later became the forces of love between man and woman were still one force of love, and this love was directed towards earth, towards the earthly substance which was to become the physical body. Earth was the 'first love' of human beings, quite literally. And when they turned away from earthly things and were only concerned with spiritual matters, as the people of Ancient India had done, and as the members of the church of Ephesus did, they 'forgot' this first love. Christ, the divine spirit who united himself with the earth, condemns those who do not care enough for the physical world and for earthly existence.

Christ's second message is for the church of Smyrna, which is a symbol for the Persian epoch. The Persians had a more positive attitude to the earth and this shows itself in the beginnings of agriculture, of farming. The farmer, the peasant, has already a close relationship to the land, to the earth. But there exists also something else; the sense of ownership, of possession. With the desire to own earthly goods, Ahriman gets hold of the human soul, and so Christ's message contains the warning, 'Some of you will be taken prisoner by the devil' (Rev.2:10).

When souls are clinging to material goods without concern for spiritual values, they cannot after death go beyond the kamaloka stage. They cannot enter the higher spheres (devachan) and are drawn back to earth. Christ's message calls this 'the second death,' which awaits those who have succumbed to Ahriman. Charles Dickens's Christmas Carol contains a description of ghosts chained to heavy cash boxes; it is an accurate imagination of the fate of the souls who suffer the 'second death.'

Christ's third message is for the church of Pergamum, which is again meant as a symbol, this time for the third post-Atlantean epoch, the civilisations of Babylon and Egypt. The characteristic feature of Babylon and Egypt mentioned by Rudolf Steiner is usually the beginning of astronomy, but in the context of the Apocalypse we are made aware that there was something else connected with the star-lore: magic. After all, when the biodynamic farmer spreads the ash of burnt vermin on his fields at a certain position of sun and moon, he too connects astronomy with magic.

And in the Egyptian-Babylonian time astro-magical practices were common. We hear, for instance in the story of Gilgamesh and his friend Eabani, that the priests of Ishtar, who had a quarrel with the two friends, created by means of magic an epidemic disease and Eabani became one of its victims and died.

Christ's letter warns against the misuse of magic powers. But those who will not be tempted to use magic for evil purposes are promised the 'hidden manna,' which means manas, the purified astral body. And souls that have attained purity from evil, selfish desires will be given 'a white stone, with a name written on the stone which no one knows except him who receives it' (Rev.2:17). The name is 'I' and the 'white stone' refers to the Holy Grail. The magic of the Grail is the power of transforming one's own nature. It is the 'white magic' that is given to mankind by Christ.

The fourth message is addressed to the church of Thyatira, which stands as a symbol for the Greco-Roman period. This is the time when the souls become wholly at home on earth. A consequence of this is that the ancient clairvoyant faculties became decadent. In their place, however, a new faculty appeared – thinking.

The letter to the church of Thyatira takes a figure from the Old Testament, Jezebel, as a symbol for the decadent clairvoyance (Rev.2:20). She was the deadly enemy of the prophet Elijah. Through her occult powers she knew that the spirit whom the Israelites called Elijah and who was the instrument of Yahweh, had as its physical bearer an outwardly insignificant personality, Naboth. At the instigation of Jezebel, Naboth was killed. Jezebel was an adherent of the cult of Baal, a religion that had become demon worship and witchcraft. She is therefore a representative for the decay of the ancient forces.

Christ's message promises to those who free themselves from these forces that they will be given the 'morning star.' Modern astronomy calls the morning star Venus, but Rudolf Steiner explains in this context that the names of Mercury and Venus were deliberately interchanged in the fifteenth century, and that therefore the correct name of the morning star is Mercury.

And as the first part of earth evolution, which made man an independent being, was ruled by Mars, so the second part should bring the power to unite the separate personalities, the power of Mercury. The Mystery of Golgotha, which took place in the Greco-Roman period, is the beginning of the Mercury-impulse, the impulse of the 'morning star.'

The faculty of logical thinking which makes its first appearance in Ancient Greece contains already the possibility of leading man in the Mercury direction, for where there is a firmly logical thought there can be no disagreement. This is, however, no more than a beginning, an 'early morning' of this unifying power. It is only when thinking becomes imbued with the light of Christ that it can become the shining, guiding star of the future evolution of mankind. The end of atavistic clairvoyance, the dawn of clear thought, this is the character of the fourth post-Atlantean period as seen by the Apocalypse.

4

The Last Three Messages
to the Churches

Rudolf Steiner describes the earth-evolution as consisting of two phases: the first is ruled by Mars, the second by Mercury. Nature provides us with a perfect image of the interaction of these two principles. Let us look at a deciduous tree in the autumn when the leaves have fallen, and the basic structure of the oak or the beech is clearly visible. There is, rising from the earth, the oneness of the mighty trunk. At a certain height this oneness becomes split into boughs, the boughs into branches and then into little twigs. Thus we see before us an unmistakable picture of the process of division and separation which is meant by the Mars principle. It is a symbol of the forces by which the original oneness of humankind became divided into races, nations, tribes and lastly separate individuals.

But the tree has more to say. The crown of an oak or a beech is not some odd, accidental shape; it tries to become a sphere, a globe, an image of the vault of the heavens above. And in that spherical shape, all the many branches and twigs which have grown in all directions are encompassed and form together a new and higher unity. One could not invent a better picture for the Mercury principle – for the cosmic power that came to earth with the Mystery of Golgotha and which bestows unity without diminishing the diversity of human beings. If one looks at a tree in this way the abstract concept Mars-Mercury becomes a living reality and one begins to realise the wisdom of the ancient myth of the Norsemen which spoke of the world-ash Yggdrasil, a tree which is the whole world.

Although Rudolf Steiner speaks about the Mars-Mercury forces in the context of the fourth post-Atlantean epoch – the Greco-Roman civilisation – the problems posed by them go far beyond this particular period of history.

Even our own time, the fifth post-Atlantean epoch, is a period of confrontation between Mars and Mercury. The Western world, with its emphasis on personal freedom and with an economic system based on ruthless competition, bears the stamp of the Mars principle. The Communist countries of the East, which tend to regard the individual as part of the community and enforce an artificial unity, represent a distortion of the Mercury principle.

The opposing demands of personal freedom and subordination of the individual to the needs of the community are indeed at the root of the social problems of our time. In the past this contradiction was resolved by the group-spirits. These higher beings, working through the blood, provided the bonds which unified the separate individuals.

What is to take their place? It can only be a spiritual power, and this power reveals itself in the message to the church of Sardis, which is the symbol for our epoch, the epoch of the consciousness soul. This message, meant for our own time, contains 'the words of him who has the seven spirits of God and the seven stars' (Rev.3:1). He is the Christ. The seven spirits of God are the seven members of the human being as set out in Theosophy, and the seven stars are the seven stages of evolution as described in Esoteric Science (GA 13). This is Rudolf Steiner's interpretation. We are not used to seeing in these fundamental concepts of anthroposophy more than the first steps in the study of spiritual science. The interpretation given here, which links these concepts with Christ, should make us revise this superficial view. We can find words by

Rudolf Steiner that can guide us in this direction (Cosmic and Human Metamorphoses, lecture of Feb 6, 1917):

> The Christ is, as he has said himself, with us always, until the end of time, and what we learn today through spiritual science is his language ... and in as much as we achieve the speaking of this language in the depths of our souls, in as much will it happen that Christ stands beside us and gives us answers to our questions.

Anthroposophy is a language, a thought-language, and the language of Christ. Through our word-languages, the languages we learn to speak as children, we are still connected with the national group-souls. The thought-language of anthroposophy is for all mankind, beyond all national groups. It is the spirit of mankind who communicates with us in this language and his language has the power to overcome all separation – the power of Mercury.

We should, however, not forget the qualification 'in as much as we achieve the speaking of this language in the depths of our souls.' One could add, 'In as far as we take anthroposophical concepts just as we take the thoughts and ideas of everyday life, these concepts will remain silent.' It will take quite some time before people have truly learned to speak the language of him who has the seven spirits of God and the seven stars.

It is not the case that human souls on earth today lack the inner forces necessary to learn this language. The forces are present in all of us, but they are used in the wrong direction; they are applied almost exclusively to earthly matters and to serve selfish material interests. Rudolf Steiner mentions in this context the technical achievements which serve only physical satisfactions.

To the souls who use the forces of the consciousness-soul only for material and selfish purposes the Apocalypse addresses the words, 'You have the name of being alive, and you are dead' (Rev.3:1).

The particular virtue of the consciousness-soul is objectivity, the ability to look upon facts without personal bias. It is the feature that has made the progress of modern science possible. If this objectivity is limited to the physical world it can only lead to a cold, inhuman attitude, which the Apocalypse regards as a kind of death. But if the soul can raise itself to the world of the spirit, free of subjective, personal inclinations, prejudices and assumptions, then objectivity opens the soul to the light of the spirit. The souls who can achieve this are promised in the Apocalypse that they will be dressed in white clothes – the colour of the pure spirit.

The calm, unemotional, matter-of-fact language in which Rudolf Steiner interprets the dramatic images of the Apocalypse is an example of the difference between the fifth age in which we live and the fourth when the Apocalypse was written. This sober language of anthroposophy is already the 'white garments' mentioned in the fifth message of Christ.

The sixth letter is addressed to the church of Philadelphia. Here the name already indicates the nature of the sixth post-Atlantean epoch which is meant by this letter – Philadelphia means brotherly love. The bearers of this impulse for brotherhood will be the Slavonic races, in particular the Russians. It is not accidental that in the twentieth century a demonic distortion of this impulse, Communism, held sway in this region of the world.

Communism regards the self as a threat to the life of a community and therefore uses every means to suppress it. But only the self, or I, can receive moral intuitions and only moral intuitions can unite people in a truly human community. The self is the key to the development of manas, the spirit-self that is necessary to bring to mankind 'Philadelphia'.

The Apocalypse uses a symbol for the self; ego; it uses the term 'key of David' (Rev.3:7), which is the esotericist's name for the six-pointed star. That some modern state uses it as a national symbol is here irrelevant – the six-pointed star is an esoteric symbol and it was used by the Rosicrucians in a special way. One has to imagine the lower triangle raised and the upper triangle lowered and then one has to stand with the arms stretched up along the lines of the triangle which is now up, and the legs spread along the lines of the triangle which is now down. Both triangles overlap in a small rhombus-shaped area around the navel. And one meditates the words 'gravity pulls downwards, light radiates upwards.' Where the triangles overlap one feels the self in the balance between light and gravity. In this balance between light and gravity there is also the balance between community and individuality. The key of David, the self is indeed the key to the social order of the future.

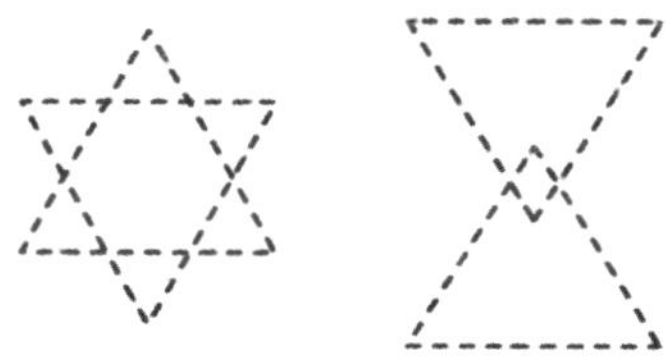

Six-pointed star

We have previously spoken about the separating forces of Mars and the uniting forces of Mercury. In the age of Philadelphia the two will be balanced. In the following age, the seventh post-Atlantean epoch, the Mars-principle will come to the fore and will lead to the 'War of All against All' and so to the end of the whole post-Atlantean cycle.

In this seventh epoch only a small group will preserve and even intensify the brotherly love of the previous epoch. They will be gathered around a great spiritual leader who is called the Amen. He is the individuality who, once before, in ancient Atlantis, led a small group away from a doomed continent to make a new start. At the time of the War of All against All he will again lead his followers to a new beginning, to form a nucleus for a new cycle. It is no accident that the name of the Atlantis leader Manes has – apart from the final 'S' – the same letters as Amen. It is an indication that it is the same being who begins and ends the post-Atlantean cycle.

5

The Unicorn and the Lion

In order to come to an understanding of the evolution of the human being one has to grasp concepts that are more complicated than those of natural science. One of these concepts could be called the principle of 'gaining something by divesting oneself of something.' A very illuminating example of this principle occurred at an early stage of earth evolution.

At that stage the astral body still contained all the animal forces that human beings had brought over from the Ancient Moon. The ferocity of the tiger, the greed of the hyena as well as the cowardice of the rabbit streamed and pulsed in the astral body. Through the deeds of higher beings these crude astral forces were 'pushed out' or externalised and so there arose the astrality of the animal world. The animals bear the astrality of which human beings have divested themselves, and through this pushing-out process the human astral body is of a much higher order and of a much finer nature than the crude astrality of the animals. It is a process that the gods have guided up to a certain point but have not completed – the completion has to be brought about by man himself.

One of the last deeds the gods performed for the human astral body occurred in the second half of the Atlantean period of evolution. The astrality that the gods removed from man – the astrality that was 'pushed out' on this occasion – was used in the formation of an animal species which had not existed before, the horse. And what man gained by getting rid of this astrality was intelligence, the beginning of human intelligence.

This statement of spiritual science raises the question: why the horse? What is there about the horse that makes it, as it were, the counterpart of intelligence?

The etheric body of present-day man coincides in the region of the head with the physical head. In man the etheric part of the head is within the boundaries of the physical head – this is not the case with the animals. Rudolf Steiner speaks, for instance, of the beautiful etheric forms flowing around the elephant's trunk. He also mentions the 'marvellous formation' outside the horse's head.

At an earlier stage of evolution man too had an etheric head that extended beyond the physical head. And as long as this was the case, people had natural clairvoyant faculties just as the animals still have. But gradually, in the course of evolution, human beings drew in the etheric head and the last part of the etheric head was drawn in during the later part of the Atlantean period. This last part of the etheric body to be drawn in was in the region of the middle of the forehead. When it was pulled inside the physical head the ancient clairvoyance ceased and the development of intelligence began. When the last etheric part became an inner organ, it became the two-petalled lotus flower. It is also the first etheric organ to be freed from the physical head in esoteric development.

What kept this etheric part outside the physical head, until the drawing-in took place, were certain astral forces, and human beings had to be relieved of these forces before the drawing-in could be accomplished. The horse species became the bearer of these forces, which constitute what Rudolf Steiner calls the 'marvellous formation' outside the horse's head. This formation cannot be seen with physical eyes, but people who retained some vestiges of the ancient clairvoyance spoke about it and so there arose the legend of the 'unicorn.'

The unicorn is a horse-like creature with a horn in the middle of the forehead. The legends connected with this mythical creature show its connection with the development of human intelligence. The fable describes the unicorn as a terribly fierce animal that cannot be caught or tamed; but when a pure virgin comes into the forest, the unicorn will lie down before her and lay its head in her lap. Intelligence is indeed a dangerous, ferocious beast and the modern era has witnessed the destruction wrought by intelligence in nature, in social life and in human relations. The pure virgin who can tame the rampant beast is Sophia, the Divine Wisdom.

In the Middle Ages the ancient imaginations were 'codified', they became abstract symbols, but even these abstractions reveal something of the esoteric knowledge that once existed. As the unicorn is the symbol of intelligence, so the lion was regarded as the symbol of faith, because religious faith springs from the heart. And when the royal coat of arms of the United Kingdom is supported on one side by the unicorn and on the other by the lion, the two beasts signify intelligence and faith. One could regard this image as an indication of the task of the consciousness-soul – that intelligence should illuminate faith and that faith should bring warmth to cold intelligence. That, in fact, the two are at present irreconcilable is part of the tragedy of our time. Without anthroposophy the lion and the unicorn cannot be reconciled.

We have seen that something had to be 'pushed out' from human nature so that man could develop intelligence, and the forces that were pushed out were given a new abode in the horse species. This happened in the second half of the Atlantean period.

A similar process is beginning in our age, but this time it is not the gods who do the pushing out, and it is not a new animal species that will give a home to the unwanted forces. Rudolf Steiner called that process now beginning, the 'confrontation with evil'. Human beings have to put the forces of evil outside themselves, drive them out. But those who will receive them are not animals, they are also human beings, people who feel no objection to evil as long as it serves their selfish ends. This time the pushing out will result in a splitting-up of humankind and the result will be a 'good race' and an 'evil race'. It is simply the next variation of the theme we have discussed: progress can only be made by pushing out what hinders the progress. But what is being pushed out must find its proper place.

We can find in nature a beautiful representation of this law. In order to form its delicate petals the rose has to 'push out' the hardening forces and so has to grow thorns. Without the thorns there could not be the wonderful blossom of the rose. What the thorns are for the rose, so are the forces of evil in man. And if we understand what nature wants to say to us with the thorns of the rose, we will also understand why Christ had to wear a crown of thorns.

6

The Four Riders of the Apocalypse

The symbolic language of the Apocalypse represents intelligence in the image of the horse. But there are different kinds of intelligence or, rather, different stages in the development of intelligence and these stages are indicated in the Apocalypse by horses of different colours.

Each of the four horses described in the vision of John refers to a past and to a future stage of mankind's evolution. In the past intelligence was instinctive; it was given to man by higher beings. In the future the same forms of intelligence will have to be gained consciously through our own efforts.

The past stages to which the horses refer are the first four epochs of civilisation after the end of Atlantis: the Indian, Persian, Egyptian and Greco-Roman periods. The four forms of intelligence developed instinctively in those times will, however, reappear as conscious achievements after the end of all the seven post-Atlantean periods. This is the connection between past and future represented by the four riders of the Apocalypse.

We have now to consider each of the horses and its rider. The particular kind of intelligence mankind developed instinctively in the Ancient Indian epoch would hardly be recognised as 'intelligence' by modern man. It was not concerned with the outside world but with the processes of digestion and reproduction inside the human organisation. Man possessed at that time an understanding of the spiritual nature of processes of which we know only the physical side. The spiritual power active in digestion and reproduction is the Moon, and to this refers the crescent shaped weapon carried by the first rider, the bow (Rev.6:2). His horse is white like the silvery light of the Moon. Of this ancient knowledge there remains only one witness, the sacrament of communion in the churches. Partaking of bread and wine is, in this ritual, not a mere physical but also a spiritual process.

The cow is the animal with the most highly developed digestive system and 'chewing the cud' is for this animal more than a mere physical experience. If one understands how in Ancient India human intelligence related to the digestive process one can also understand that the Hindu tradition still regards the cow as sacred.

In the Persian epoch intelligence was still partly directed to inner, organic functions, but partly also to the world outside man. This duality is characteristic of the rhythmic system – breathing and the blood circulation. At this stage intelligence is divided between polarities: inhaling and exhaling, systole and diastole of the heart. This division is expressed by the weapon in the hand of the second rider – a sword – and his mount is red, the colour of blood (Rev.6:4).

In a later period the Greek philosopher Heraclitus expressed the wisdom of the Persian epoch in the words 'war is the father of all things.' This saying does not refer to 'war' in the usual sense, but to the polarities that exist in all there is in the world: light-darkness, summer-winter, thinking-will, etc. The Chinese yin-yang philosophy has its origin in the soul-attitude of the Persian epoch. Goethe's theory of colour, which sees in every colour a struggle between light and darkness, represents a reawakening of the intelligence of the rider on the red horse.

The third post-Atlantean civilisation flourished in North Africa and the Middle East, in Egypt and Babylon. Now intelligence, having passed through the digestive and rhythmic systems, takes hold of the nervous system which, by its nature, is directed towards the outer world, the world of the senses. A consequence of this is that the spiritual world sinks into darkness, and intelligence, in order to cope with the sense world, uses as its tool the power of numbers, calculation, mathematics.

This was the time when writing was invented and so the living word was replaced by abstract symbols. It was also the time when the Babylonians learned to calculate the movements of the planets (astronomy) and the Egyptians calculated the area of each peasant's field (geometry). The intelligence which learned to measure time and space is indicated by the tool in the third horseman's hand; a pair of scales. And the darkening of the spiritual world is expressed by the black colour of his steed (Rev.6:5).

Since all evolution follows the same laws it is not surprising that the development of the child shows parallels to the three stages that have just been described. For the child in the first years of life the experience of eating is very different from that of the adult. When the little child eats something sweet, the taste is not only in the mouth but pervades the whole being. The young child enjoys eating altogether with body and soul and so comes quite close to the way in which eating was experienced in ancient India.

In the second seven-year period the child needs rhythm and rhythmical movements in his life. This is also the time when education should strengthen and appeal to the heart forces, to feeling.

In the third seven-year period, from fourteen to twenty-one, the adolescent of the present era cannot feel the connection with the stars, which was the compelling force behind Babylonian astronomy, but he still feels the need for guiding stars, which means the example of men and women whose lives were devoted to ideals. Ideals are the 'guiding stars' of the present age, and the adolescent whose education does not inspire idealism will grasp surrogates: pop stars, gang leaders, political extremists.

The three stages in the evolution of intelligence as they can be seen in the Indian, Persian and Egyptian civilisations correspond also to the archetypes we have discussed previously. The Indian civilisation corresponds to the Bull, the animal with the most highly developed digestive system. The Persian civilisation corresponds to the animal with the best developed rhythmic system, the lion. The Egyptian civilisation is an expression of the Eagle forces, which work in the formation of the brain and the nervous system. The veneration of the Horus Falcon by the pharaohs is a sign that this connection was known and understood.

Once the relation of these three epochs to Bull, Lion and Eagle is understood, it becomes clear that the next stage, the Greco-Roman civilisation, corresponds to the fourth archetype, to Man. This is one side of the fourth epoch; that intelligence becomes human – it is no longer something bestowed by higher beings. This is the reason why 'mythology' as a way of understanding the world comes to an end, and 'philosophy' begins.

But there is also another side to this development. In a lecture Rudolf Steiner tells us that the Greeks were quite aware that the intelligence they had could only comprehend what was dead, lifeless, a corpse (Education as a Force for Social Change, lecture of Aug 16, 1919). Only clairvoyant vision – either through initiation in the mysteries or as an atavistic remnant of the past – could give an understanding of life and how life-forces worked in the world. Intelligence had only the power to understand what was without life. And this is confirmed by the Apocalypse for the fourth horseman – the symbol of the Greco-Roman period is death and the colour of his horse is called 'pale,' which means the colour of a corpse (Rev.6:8). If we consider the two symbolic images referring to this civilisation, Man and the rider whose name is Death, we can understand that this was the time when Christ became man and overcame death.

The theme of intelligence is central to the whole Apocalypse. It is also the main theme in Rudolf Steiner's last message to anthroposophists, the Michael Letters. Behind the scenes of the physical world a war is waged for this thing we call 'intelligence' and both the Apocalypse and the Michael Letters try to bring it home to us, that the way we use, or misuse, or do not use at all, the intelligence forces in us, will decide the future of humankind's evolution. For our age, the fifth post-Atlantean period, there is in the Apocalypse no rider or horse. Next we shall try to understand why this is so.

7

The 'Christened' Intelligence

The post-Atlantean cycle consists of seven epochs which end with the War of All against All. Then a new cycle begins in which the 'intelligences' of the previous seven epochs will reappear in a higher form. What this means can be understood by considering the description of life after death given by Rudolf Steiner (Supersensible Man, Nov 14, 1923).

Immediately after death the human form of the previous life persists for a short time, but soon a change takes place. The form loses the head, the head dissolves whilst at the same time a new 'physiognomy' appears in the middle and lower parts of the spirit form. And this new countenance that is acquired after death shows with relentless truthfulness the moral, or immoral, nature of the soul. What was, during earth life, good or evil within us is turned outside and made manifest. We shall look as we morally are.

At the present stage of evolution this 'turning inside out' takes place only after death, in the astral world. But humanity is moving towards a future when the laws of the astral world will be reflected in the sense world. This will be the situation in the new cycle after the War of All against All, when good and beautiful, evil and ugly will be synonymous.

In that future new cycle there will first arise the intelligence of the Indian epoch, and the moral or immoral use people made of it will be written in their faces. It will be similar with the particular forms of intelligence developed in the Persian, Egyptian and Greco-Roman epochs. One after another they will emerge, and whether they were used for good or for evil will be made manifest. In the past people owed their looks mainly to heredity. In the future, after the War of All against All, one's looks will be the result of one's own deeds. The four riders described in the Apocalypse are symbols of this future.

The intelligences of the first four epochs of the post-Atlantean cycle are symbolised in the Apocalypse by horsemen to indicate that intelligence was then still to some extent guided by higher beings. This is not the case with the fifth post-Atlantean epoch in which we live, or with the following ones. Beginning with this present epoch of the consciousness-soul we are on our own, and no divine rider holds the reins of our specific 'horse'. It is up to each one of us where we go and at what pace.

What is the nature of the intelligence of our time? In the educational lecture already mentioned, in which Rudolf Steiner links the intelligence of the Greco-Roman epoch with death, he goes on to characterise the intelligence of the present age (Education as a Force, Aug 16, 1919). It is still bound up with death but now something else is coming into it, something that is already discernible but which will become even worse as time goes on. The direction that intelligence now takes leads us to this: that man will – precisely through intelligence – come to accept what is false as true and what is wrong as right, and that, just through intelligence, he will only be led to do what is evil. Falsehood and error in knowledge and wrongness and evil in actions, these are the goals to which the worldly intelligence of our time leads, to which it must lead.

There is a famous engraving by the German artist Albrecht Dürer, showing a knight in armour riding a horse. In front of the horse stands death, at the back of it stands a horrible-looking devil. It is a very apt image of the intelligence of our epoch. Dürer, who lived at the beginning of this epoch, saw in his artistic vision what was coming.

Others, too, have a faint feeling for the nature of intelligence in our time but react wrongly to the threat. Rudolf Steiner

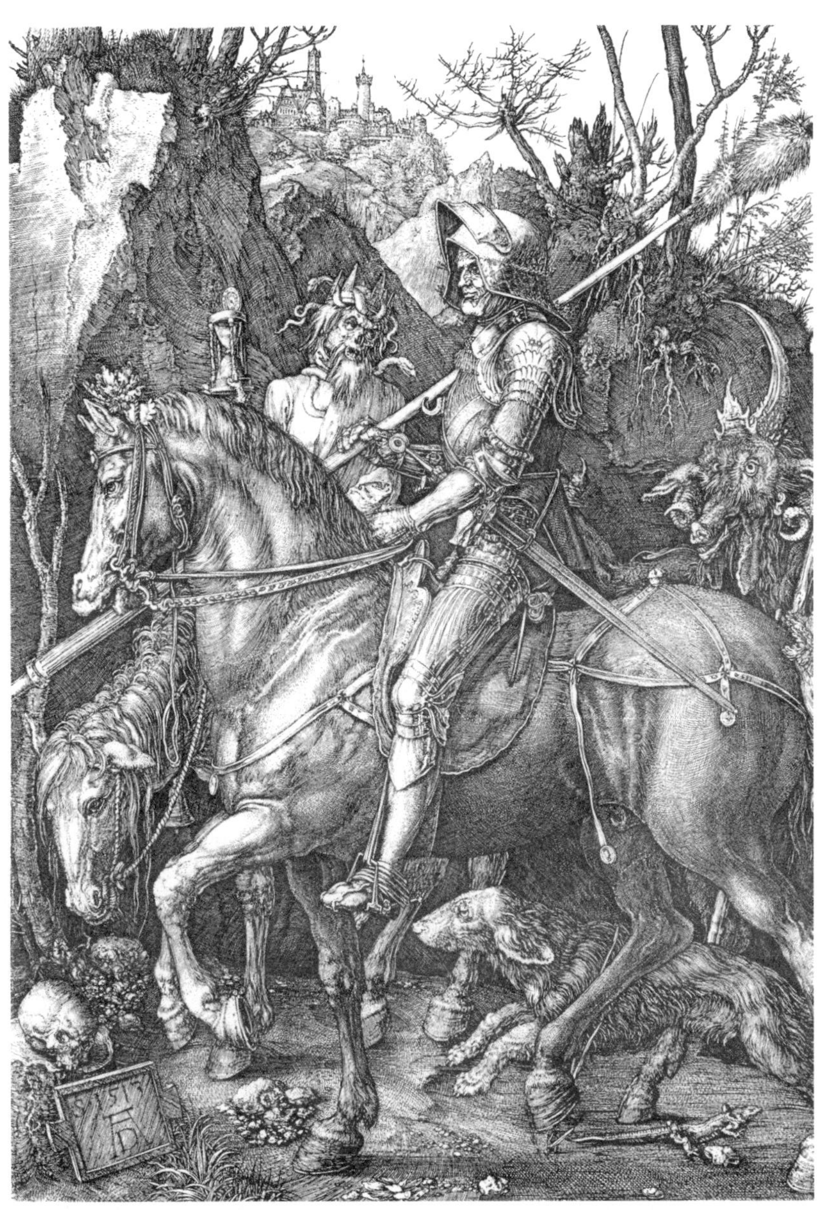

Albrecht Dürer, Knight between Death and the Devil. 1513

speaks in the lecture about people who, out of such feelings, let their intelligence go to sleep and prefer to exist with a blunted mind. But to remain stupid avails nothing. Man should and must make use of intelligence, but this can only be beneficial and wholesome if this intelligence is, in Rudolf Steiner's word, *durchchristet*, meaning 'imbued with the Christ-spirit'. This 'Christ-ening' of intelligence is in the present age possible through work on the contents of anthroposophy.

One might add to these remarks made by Rudolf Steiner that a thoughtless acceptance of anthroposophical doctrines would not meet the demands made by his call for a Christening of intelligence. He also places a heavy responsibility on teachers when he tells them in this lecture, 'One has to be conscious when teaching that it is one's duty to bring to every child the possibility of finding in the course of life the Christ impulse within the soul, to find the power of a spiritual rebirth within.'

In the epoch of the consciousness-soul, intelligence can either become a force, not for evil but of evil, or it can be transformed into a force of good. The change from being to begin with morally neutral to something essentially evil is so gradual – it creeps up so silently on mankind – that people just do not notice what is going on. This is demonstrated by the remarkable example given by Rudolf Steiner in these Apocalypse lectures.

He refers to the development of the banking system. At the beginning of the nineteenth century the Frankfurt banker, Mayer Rothschild, sent his sons to the capitals of Europe, to London, Paris, Naples and Vienna. They started branches of their father's Frankfurt bank and did very well. This was the first international banking concern and it was the work of the personal enterprise of the members of this family. In Rudolf Steiner's time, two generations later, banking had completely changed. It had become impersonal, a vast machine encompassing the globe; it had become a 'system' in which the single personality is only a replaceable part. Capitalism – and this is what the banking system stands for – had become an organisation that has no concern for human individuality and can only destroy it.

The same is true of socialism, which began with personalities who felt strongly about the social injustice brought about by the Industrial Revolution (Marx, Lassalle, Engels). What followed later from this impulse were socialist systems in which there existed neither justice nor freedom. Political parties, educational institutions, the mass-media, the multinational corporations, are all systems which work in the direction of destroying and devaluing the human personality – and this means in the direction of evil. In the past, communities were held together by 'group spirits', by higher spiritual beings who guided the souls in their care towards true progress. These good group spirits have withdrawn, and in their place there are new group spirits, the demonic powers who are the spiritual reality behind the systems whose aim is to kill and to crush altogether the human personality.

And what the seer John beholds as the symbol of our own age is not a horseman; it is something different. He sees the bodies of men who have been killed at the altars where they wanted to worship, and the souls of the slain are crying out for retribution (Rev.6:9). It is the symbol for the assassination of the personal element in human nature. In this epoch it is only the Christened intelligence that can keep the human individuality alive. And the souls who have striven and worked for this Christened intelligence are comforted. Just as the first four epochs of the present cycle will rise again in the next cycle, so too will the intelligence of our epoch.

The Christened intelligence will then show itself outwardly. The Apocalypse expresses this by saying that these souls will be given 'white garments', Whether men have developed the individual Christened intelligence or have allowed their intelligence to conform to the systems, and so to be taken over by the group-demons, will be seen outwardly in their appearance. One could say that with our studies of anthroposophy we are creating the forms of our bodies in the next cycle.

The sixth post-Atlantean epoch, the one which follows the present age of the consciousness soul, is destined to develop manas or spirit-self which means the purified astral body. As the word 'astral' indicates, it is the part of our being that is related to the stars. This intelligence of the coming epoch will therefore be directed towards an understanding of the connection between man and the cosmos.

This intelligence, too, will rise up again in the sixth epoch of the next cycle, but transformed. What this transformation will mean is indicated by Rudolf Steiner when he said that human souls began their incarnations in physical bodies in the Lemurian cycle, and during Atlantis and the post-Atlantean epochs they incarnated again and again, but that this law of reincarnation does not go on indefinitely. In the course of the sixth cycle after the War of All against All, the souls who have made the necessary progress will cease to incarnate in physical bodies. Their lowest part will be the etheric body. This means that man will not only know his connection with the cosmos but will know himself as a cosmic being just as he knows himself now as an earthly being.

Once we understand this change in human consciousness we can also understand the symbolic language in which the Apocalypse refers to it. The physical aspect of sun, moon and stars as we see them today will disappear as man awakens to the spiritual powers behind them. The Apocalypse describes it by saying that the sun will be like a black sack, the moon red as blood, and that the stars will fall from heaven.

The seventh post-Atlantean epoch will bring the War of All against All. When the intelligence of this period of disaster will reappear at the end of the following cycle, the division of mankind into souls who have advanced sufficiently to no longer need physical bodies, and those who cannot free themselves from earth will be complete. According to the Apocalypse, one third of mankind will have reached the higher stage, one third will still have the possibility to reach it later, but one third will be lost and will not be able to take part in the further evolution of human souls.

Freedom must necessarily include the possibility of refusing to advance in accordance with the true spirit of mankind. The last third of mankind mentioned in the Apocalypse are souls who have made this choice.

8

Evolution and Involution

The number seven figures very prominently in the Apocalypse: seven candlesticks, seven letters, seven trumpets, and so on. There seem to be no end of things that come in sevens. In the ninth lecture the theme of 'seven' is taken up by Rudolf Steiner. He places before us a scheme of evolution, from Ancient Saturn to the future Vulcan, which comprises seven times seven times seven stages. He was well aware how abstract such a purely numerical system is and therefore provided later the images of the seven seals and the seven capitals as they are called, which were eventually incorporated in the pillars of the first Goetheanum.

It is necessary to get away from the mere counting up to seven and to come to living pictures that can elucidate the qualitative aspect of sevenfoldness as distinct from the meaningless quantity. We can find a way to such pictures by using an approach suggested by Rudolf Steiner in lectures on art, even though what he said there is in no way connected with seven or any other number. The suggestion made in that lecture was to take a look at the physically visible form of a flower. What can be observed is a static form.

But this form is the result of active forces. The form is the dead image of dynamic processes, of movement. So the next step is to go in one's mind from the dead form to the streams of forces which created the form. Instead of the physical details, leaves, stem, petals, one has to visualise moving, flowing forces. It has to be mentioned that these 'force streams'

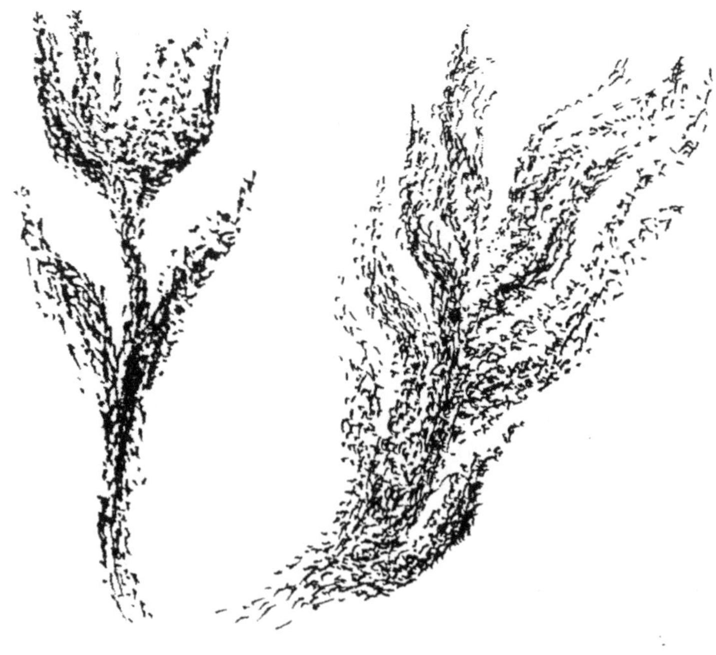

A static plant form, and a dynamic plant form

are not mere fantasy. They are real and constitute the plant's etheric body.

Then follows the next step: the force streams could not possibly move in a chaotic fashion. There is some underlying principle that directs and determines and co-ordinates their movements. And if one tries to grasp this unifying principle one comes to a 'gesture.' This is the expression used by Rudolf Steiner in this context. The forces do not just flow anywhere, anyhow, but have a general tendency; they are part of a 'gesture', which is, in fact, the gesture common to all plant life.

It is the same gesture that children use instinctively when they are about to receive something. It is also the gesture used in olden times when praying to the gods. Rudolf Steiner called it the gesture of Bitte, which means both prayer and request. A gesture is not a meaningless form – it says something. The

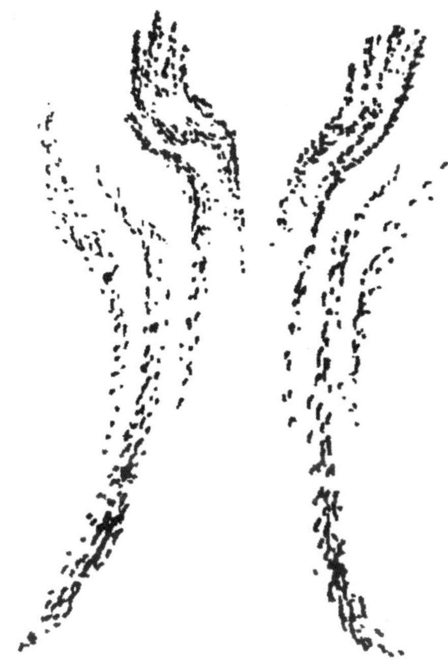

The 'gesture' of a plant

gesture of the flower is a prayer and a request. It is the Earth Spirit which turns in every flower to the sun, requesting light.

So we have three stages in this contemplation of the flower. First the form, then the force streams that create the form, and third the gesture that directs the flow of forces. Then there is a fourth element: the being who speaks through the gesture. But these stages are, in fact, an image of the great stages of evolution.

On Ancient Saturn there appeared the first form of the human body. It was still only a form, without life. On the Ancient Sun, the life forces entered into the form. On the Ancient Moon, the astral body was added and it brought the ability to express inner experiences (joy, fear) outwardly in movements, in gestures. On Earth the I or self enters these sheaths. In human language the self uses the physical, etheric and astral bodies for its own purposes. In future stages of evolution the self will gain complete mastery of the three sheaths.

It can now be seen that in the three stages of the contemplation of the flower, we have a picture of both the past and the future evolution of man and thus of the meaning of 'seven', The self stands in the middle of this evolution. And just as the Earth Spirit turns in a gesture of prayer to the sun, so the self, in its true, inner nature, is an unceasing prayer for the light of the spiritual sun, the Christ. And the gesture performed by countless blossoms is an image of the nature of our innermost being, the self.

From the concept of the seven stages there arises a recognition that there are really two phases in the development of man and the world. Rudolf Steiner calls these 'evolution' and 'involution' and between them there is a 'gap' – the place of the human self.

Here too the flower offers the right image. The chalice of the blossom signifies a prayer for the light. What happens after the request is granted? There comes the formation of the fruit and within the fruit the seed. In the seed the whole life of the plant is concentrated and has no longer any visible manifestation. It becomes an inner power. What we see from spring to summer is 'evolution' – what takes place from summer to autumn is 'involution'.

In the schools of esoteric knowledge, the symbol for evolution and involution was a pair of spirals that almost meet in one point – but there remains a gap. It is not an accident that these two spirals are also the symbol of the zodiac sign Cancer, the sign of summer, when the life forces of the flower begin to draw inwards, when evolution becomes involution.

Up to the Greco-Roman epoch, humankind was still on the path of evolution. From then onwards we have to strive for involution. In the middle of the Greco-Roman epoch there is a 'gap'. In that gap the Mystery of Golgotha took place.

Another symbol of the sevenfoldness is the seven-branched candlestick that one sees in churches of the Christian

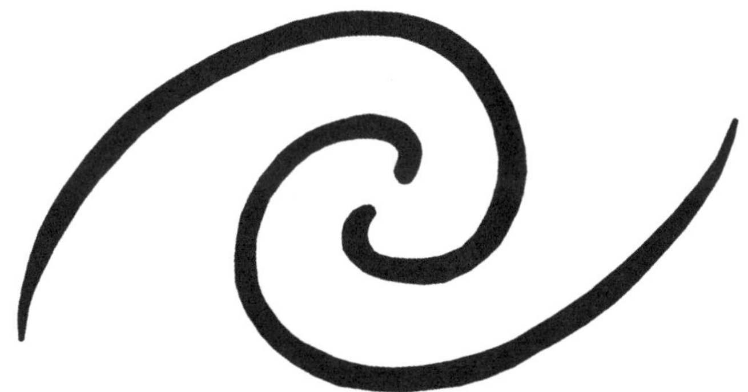

The double spiral, symbol of evolution and involution

Community but which is of much more ancient origin. It is an essential part of every Jewish synagogue and goes back to Moses and the seven days of creation in Genesis. The branches are in pairs, except the one in the middle. The middle candle represents the 'gap'– the self.

There is still one more aspect of 'seven' to be considered. On Ancient Saturn the first human form came into being. On Ancient Sun the form was given life. On Ancient Moon inner experiences began that represent the first kind of awareness, of consciousness. But these three concepts – form, life, consciousness – are fundamental to Rudolf Steiner's scheme of evolution as set out in the Apocalypse lectures. We are told that there are seven conditions of form, each divided into seven kingdoms of life, each of which is subdivided into seven stages of consciousness. This makes seven times seven times seven, which equals three hundred and forty three phases of evolution.

All three are present all the time, but on Saturn there was more emphasis on form, during the Sun period life was more to the foreground and on Ancient Moon the accent was on awareness or consciousness. During Earth evolution all three are balanced.

What these three – form, life, consciousness – actually are, was not said in the course of the Apocalypse lectures, but was revealed to a smaller circle on a previous occasion. They are the highest spiritual powers, which the Christian tradition calls God the Father, God the Son, and God the Holy Spirit. The Holy Trinity is not something remote from our life and being, but is present in our evolution and sustains it. Every form bears witness to the Father, every living thing to the Son and any being capable of pleasure or pain manifests the Holy Spirit.

In the three past stages of evolution man was made an image of the Trinity. In the three future stages of involution man is meant to unite his inner being with the powers of the Trinity. This is the purpose of man's existence. And the number seven expresses this purpose.

All the sevens in tradition and legend, the seven petitions in the Lord's Prayer, the seven days of the week, the seven ravens and the seven dwarves, the seven tones of the musical scale and the seven colours of the rainbow – and all the sevens in the Apocalypse – they are meant to remind us again and again that there is a meaning and purpose in our existence.

9

Jachim and Boaz

Anyone who reads the Apocalypse of John, the last book of the New Testament, is confronted with a flood of images, most of them terrifying and all of them practically incomprehensible. There have been many attempts at interpreting these mysterious symbolic descriptions but only an initiate, like Rudolf Steiner, could lift the veil which hides the secrets of this book. Yet even he did not explain every verse and chapter in this work. He chose certain key images for the Theosophical Congress in Munich in 1907 and had them painted by a not very talented member. These are the seven seals to which Rudolf Steiner referred in his lectures on this occasion. What he said is fundamental for an understanding of the Apocalypse. This is especially the case with the fourth seal.

John describes how he saw a being whose face was like the sun, and his legs like pillars of fire (Rev.10:1). One pillar is red and stands in the waters of the ocean; the other is blue and stands on firm earth. The being gives John a book or scroll and commands him to eat it. He obeys and the book is as sweet as honey in his mouth but it then gives him a great pain in his stomach. This image in the last book of the Bible contains, unmistakably, a reference to the first book of the Old Testament, Genesis, to the Fall of Man.

Genesis speaks of two trees, the Tree of Life and the Tree of Knowledge. In the lecture given at the Munich Congress in 1907 Rudolf Steiner brings these two images together (Rosicrucianism Renewed). The two pillars in the vision of

John are symbols for the two kinds of blood in the human organism: the light red arterial blood and the bluish red venous blood. The 'red' blood carries oxygen from the lungs to all parts of the body, the 'blue' blood carries the used air, carbon dioxide, to the lungs.

The red blood is – so Rudolf Steiner explained – the Tree of Knowledge in us. The blue blood is the Tree of Life which has, however, through the Fall of Man, become the Tree of Death. What we breathe out, carbon dioxide, is not life-giving like oxygen, but life-destroying. We owe it to the plant world that the oxygen content of the air is continuously renewed. The plants take in the carbon dioxide that we breathe out and break it up into carbon and oxygen. They retain the carbon and return the oxygen to the air. However, the plants can only perform this chemical process with the help of the sunlight; it does not take place at night. For science photosynthesis by plants is still a mystery. It would solve all energy problems if we could harness the sunlight.

In schools of true esotericism there has always existed a knowledge of this sun mystery. Rudolf Steiner revealed in this lecture that man is destined to accomplish in a still distant future what is now only possible for the plant: he will be able to awaken the inner sun forces in himself and to break up the carbon dioxide in his organism, retain the carbon and return the oxygen to the air. Rudolf Steiner added: 'When man can do consciously what the plants are doing unconsciously, he develops within his own being the chalice of the Holy Grail.'

In the Esoteric School lectures Rudolf Steiner speaks of 'masters' like Christian Rosenkreutz, who have already reached this stage. They do not need any food except occasionally some water; they do not fall ill and they do not die until they themselves decide it is time to seek a new incarnation. What contemporaries of the Count of Saint Germain report about him seems to bear out this description.

Such a being breathes out oxygen as well as in; his arterial blood is the same as the venous blood. In other words, the Tree of Knowledge and the Tree of Life are one in him, as they were in man before the Fall.

Through the Fall we have lost this unity. One consequence of this is that for us Knowledge and Life are not one. Even when we know what we should do, we are often incapable of acting and living in accordance with this knowledge. This realisation brings us back to the fourth seal and to the symbol of the little book that the Sun-being gives John to eat. It is sweet in John's mouth but gives him a great pain in his belly. This is a very drastic image, but the experience to which it refers is only too well known to us.

Who of us has not experienced joy and satisfaction with one or another content of spiritual science? But when we ask ourselves how much of this precious knowledge has become life in us, how much of it lives in our soul and in our actions, then we have to admit it is only very little and that most of what we have read lies, as it were, undigested in us. If we are honest with ourselves in this respect then the discrepancy between the Tree of Knowledge and the Tree of Life in us becomes a reality. And we can also understand the meaning of the book that is sweet in the mouth but gives great trouble to the stomach.

It is not every kind of knowledge that leads to such a realisation. Neither mathematics nor biology would give anyone a twinge of conscience, but any esoteric or occult knowledge (and that is why it was 'occult', which means hidden from most people) demands the whole human being and this is the reason for the stomach ache. In our time this knowledge can no longer be kept secret; on the contrary, mankind needs it. But this means also that mankind as a whole will have to know this kind of 'pain in the belly'.

What is this little book in the fourth seal? We have seen it before. There is a book with a Lamb on it in the second seal. There is the same book again, open, in the third seal. Now, in the fourth seal, the Sun-being gives this same book to John who has to eat it. It is the Book of Evolution.

Up to the Mystery of Golgotha, evolution was the work

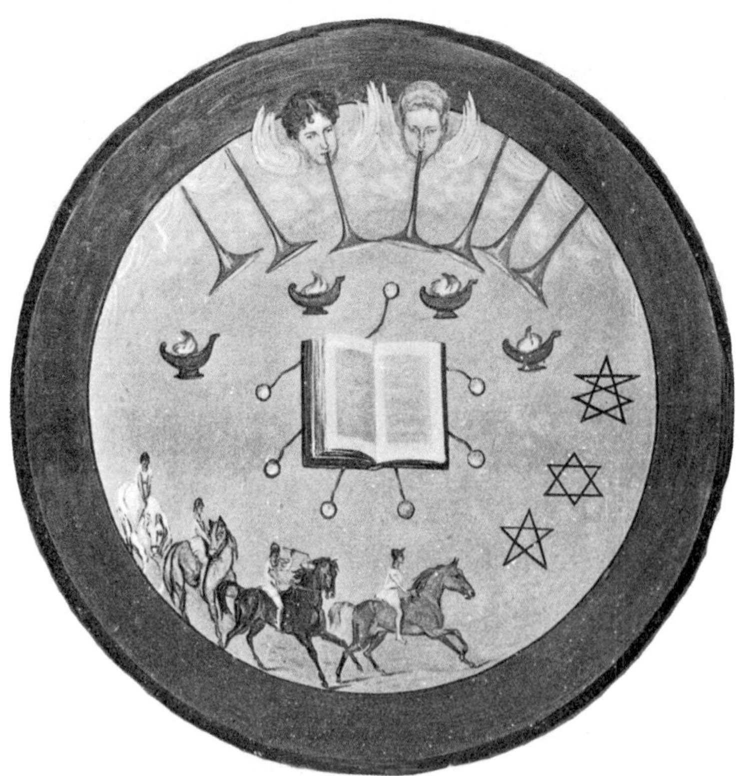

Sketch of the third seal of the Apocalypse

of the gods; it was the result of forces outside us. But from Golgotha onwards evolution becomes ever more man's own responsibility. This is the 'swallowing' of the book and the pain in the belly is the responsibility which now falls upon us. It is a part of this process that human beings have to gain control of the forces of their own physical organisation and do for themselves what now the plants do: the break-up of carbon dioxide into carbon and oxygen.

In 1916 Rudolf Steiner returned to the theme of the two pillars and this time with reference to another part of the Bible. On the fourth seal, the red pillar that stands in the sea bears the letter 'J', the blue pillar that stands on the earth has the letter

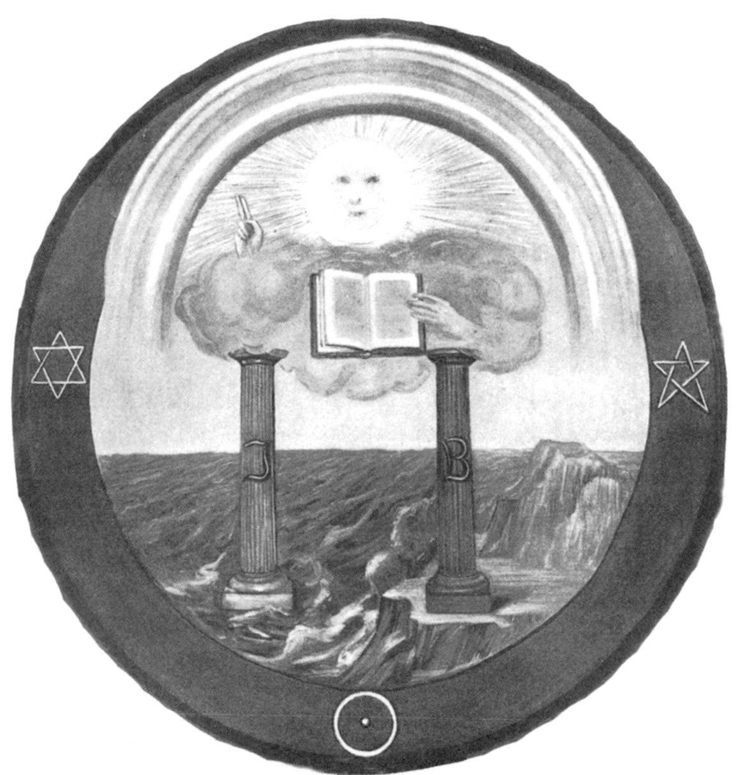

Sketch of the fourth seal of the Apocalypse

'B'. These are the initials of the words Jachim and Boaz, the names of the two pillars that stood before the Temple of King Solomon in Jerusalem. Small replicas of Jachim and Boaz are still an essential part of the furnishing of every Masonic lodge.

Rudolf Steiner spoke of these names of the pillars (Towards Imagination, June 20, 1916). The word Jachim, he explained, expresses the forces which lead man from the spiritual world to earthly existence: the forces of birth. Boaz expresses the forces which lead man from the physical world to the world of the spirit; the forces of death.

We can see from this that the forces in the red arterial blood are identical with Jachim, the forces of birth, and that the forces working in the blue venous blood are identical with Boaz, the forces of death. And we can now understand that he who has mastered the processes of the blood is also master of life and death.

Rudolf Steiner describes Jachim as the process in which the human being, descending towards birth, contracts the macrocosm so that it becomes the microcosm, the physical human being. Boaz is the process in which the microcosmic being expands at death and becomes the macrocosm. Birth and death are really a kind of slow in-breathing and out-breathing. And then Rudolf Steiner replaces the ancient Hebrew words for these processes with sentences in the language of the present age. Jachim means 'God within me' and Boaz means 'I within God'. We are born in order to find God within us; we die to find ourselves in God.

And the two sentences I have quoted were taken up again by Rudolf Steiner towards the end of his life, although without mention of the two pillars. In one of the Curative Education lectures (July 6, 1924) it is his concern that, particularly for teachers, knowledge and life become one. It is the challenge mentioned before in connection with the Tree of Knowledge and the Tree of Life. Rudolf Steiner wanted the teachers to have a 'living knowledge' and he gave them the following meditation which would help them in this direction:

> In the evening imagine a blue circle with a yellow point in the centre. Together with this image meditate on the words: God is within me.
>
> In the morning imagine a yellow circle with a blue point in the centre and with this picture meditate on the words: I am within God.

These words are, as mentioned before, the modern equivalent of Jachim and Boaz. And the meditation of the words, together with the circles, is meant to awaken in the soul the capacity for a 'living knowledge' or, in other words, a union of the Tree of Knowledge and the Tree of Life. And by working on this meditation the first step is made towards the distant goal of which Rudolf Steiner spoke at the Theosophical Congress in 1907: the goal of developing the chalice of the Holy Grail. One is on the path to the mystery of the two pillars in the fourth seal of the Apocalypse.

10

The Lamb

One of the most profound symbols in the Apocalypse is the Lamb of God. Rudolf Steiner makes only a short reference to it in these lectures, but in the second seal the Lamb is shown resting on the Book with Seven Seals. On the third seal the book is shown open and the text of the Apocalypse states that only the Lamb can open it.

The term Lamb of God appears earlier in the New Testament. It is used by John the Baptist when Jesus approaches him for the baptism. It is at this moment that John utters the words, 'Behold, the Lamb of God who takes away the sin of the world' (John 1:29). For the Jews of that time such a pronouncement had a particular significance. The most solemn festival of the year was the Day of Atonement, the day on which they fasted, repented their sins, and asked God's forgiveness. And on this day the sins of the people were, in a symbolic ritual, transferred by the priest to a goat which was then driven into the desert to die. This was the 'scapegoat', the goat upon which the people had unloaded their transgressions. For us such a notion seems ridiculous, but for the people of that time this custom was a preparation for the concept that one day there would be one who would take the sin of all mankind upon himself; the Lamb of God. Not a goat but the innocent young lamb is the image for this being.

But what is the sin that the Lamb is going to bear? We know that our personal deeds and misdeeds are written into our karma and will find their just reward in the following incarnations. These are not the sins which concern the Lamb of God.

There is, however, one sin that no individual karma can wipe out: the sin that made us separate individuals – the Fall of Man.

Without this original sin man could not have attained conscious selfhood, and with it, freedom. But with this freedom, man became at the same time cut off from the divine world, cut off from the beings and the forces of nature and, finally, cut off from fellow human beings. This is the sin from which karma cannot absolve him. In fact it is through karma that we become ever more individualised and different from each other. What is necessary if man is to retain the result of original sin (freedom and the separate distinct individuality) yet be reunited with the spirit in the cosmos, in nature, and in fellow human beings? Some being higher than man, untouched by original sin, has to take the burden of that sin upon himself, in freedom, as a deed of love. This being is Christ, the Lamb of God. He has offered himself in freedom as the 'scapegoat' for the whole of mankind.

The Rosicrucians called this aspect of the Mystery of Golgotha the Great Sacrifice. It is a sacrifice beyond our comprehension. Rudolf Steiner said once that if people understood the meaning of the 'Lamb of God who takes away the sin of the world', they would blanch.

Only in this context can we understand the wording of the last request in the Lord's Prayer. The request 'give us our daily bread' refers, as Rudolf Steiner explained, to the physical body; 'forgive us our trespasses' refers to the etheric body; 'lead us not into temptation' refers to the astral body. At the end we pray 'deliver us from evil' – and that 'evil' is the self as it has become in the course of evolution. The self could not be anything but evil if Christ had not made the Great Sacrifice and so delivered man from the evil of egohood.

There is still another mystery connected with the Lamb of God. We have on a previous occasion, in Chapter 5, spoken of a stage in human evolution when the etheric head, which had been outside the physical head, was 'drawn in' so that from then on the physical and etheric heads coincided. The centre of this process is a part of the etheric body that lies close to the pituitary gland. It is the two-petalled lotus flower. When this etheric organ was discussed previously it was in connection with the development of intelligence. Personal intelligence – as distinct from the instinctive intelligence of the animals – could only arise after the etheric forces outside the head had been drawn in and the two-petalled lotus flower had become an internal organ. But this lotus flower also has another function; it is the organ of consciousness of self. The knowledge 'I am I' is mediated by this etheric organ. When the spiritual light of this chakra is directed towards the outside world it gives rise to intelligence; when this light turns inwards it makes us aware of our egohood.

In ancient times when human beings were still under the guidance of the folk-souls, only initiates could experience consciousness of self. Such an initiate was Moses. To him God revealed himself in the fiery thorn bush as 'I AM the I AM'. What the Old Testament describes in this imagination is the awakening of ego-consciousness. As mentioned before, this is only possible through the activity of the two-petalled chakra, and that Moses had developed this supersensible organ is expressed in the tradition that depicts him with two lamb's horns on his head, as can be seen in Michelangelo's famous statue of Moses. The 'horns' of Moses are a symbol for the two-petalled chakra and for the consciousness of self, which is one of its functions. It is part of the same tradition that esoteric schools call the two-petalled chakra the Lamb.

But behind this Lamb symbol there is a cosmic connection. One of the oldest astrological traditions, and one which Rudolf Steiner confirmed, relates the human body to the twelve constellations of the zodiac. And in this correlation the head is formed by the forces of the constellation Aries, the Ram – and the highest function of the head is consciousness of self. The organ for consciousness of self, the two-petalled chakra, is quite literally the offspring of the Aries' forces, the offspring of the cosmic Ram. By calling it the Lamb the esotericists pointed to the cosmic powers whose work the two-petalled chakra is.

From the exalted cosmic realm of the zodiac, Christ, the Lamb of God, came to earth in the Greco-Roman period when the spring equinox stood in the constellation Aries, and the Mystery of Golgotha took place when the sun also stood in Aries. And what came about through the Mystery of Golgotha is this: that the 'Lamb of God, who takes away the sin of the world' can unite itself with the Lamb in man's etheric body. It means that the human consciousness of self can receive the Christ impulse; it means what St Paul expressed in the words, 'Not I, but the Christ within me' (Gal.2:20).

The Lamb symbol has led us to cosmic heights but it also opens a view into the abyss of evil. The Apocalypse of John speaks of a demonic power that stands in eternal opposition to the Lamb of God. Just as the Christ impulse wants to infuse life and movement into the two-petalled chakra (the Lamb), so the Antichrist wants to harden this etheric organ so that it develops into two rigid horns. In the Antichrist himself this is already the case. The Apocalypse hints at this by saying of this demon that he has two horns like those of a lamb (Rev.13:11). This is the reason why the esoteric sign for the Antichrist (shown by Rudolf Steiner in these lectures and given originally in the work of the medieval esotericist Agrippa von Nettesheim) is this:

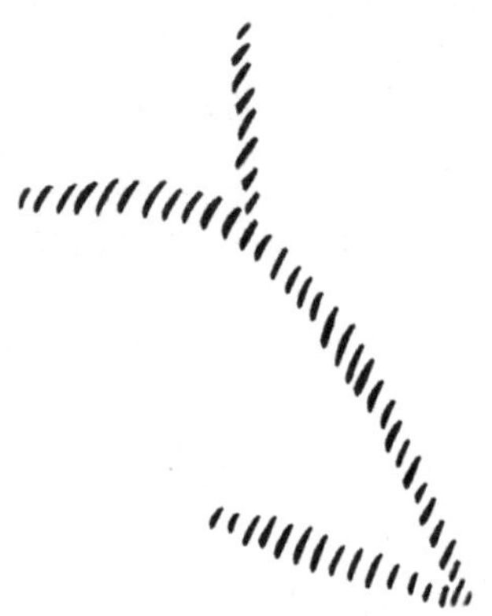

The Sorat sign

Rudolf Steiner also reveals in these lectures by what means the Antichrist will pursue his aim of making man a horned beast: by means of human intelligence. It is intelligence that will deliver man into the power of the ultimate evil, the arch-enemy of Christ.

We have seen that the faculty of intelligence awoke in man when the two-petalled chakra became 'internalised' and situated within the physical head. This chakra, the Lamb, should be freed from the physical body. This is the intention of the Christ impulse. To keep it in the physical head and to harden it into horns, that is the Antichrist impulse. And the battle for this organ, the Lamb, has already begun.

11

The Beast

Rudolf Steiner's educational lecture has already been mentioned in Chapter 7 (Education as a Force, Aug 16, 1919). It is the lecture in which he describes the future evolution of human intelligence: that it will, by its own nature, lead man into evil unless it is redeemed by the Christ impulse. Intelligence by itself can only make man an evil being. The Apocalypse tells us that the evil that lies on the path of intelligence is connected with the two-horned beast, the Antichrist. What is the nature of this evil? It is black magic.

Before we can understand what 'black magic' means, we have to consider first magic in general – the nature of magical forces, whether they are used for good or for evil purposes. It will be somewhat surprising to learn that we are using magical forces all the time.

In a lecture of the Curative Education Course (June 27, 1924) Rudolf Steiner explains what really happens when we stand up or walk. One might think that the I, or self, commands the physical body to stand up or to walk and that then the body uses its own physical forces to execute the order. This concept is completely mistaken. When we awake in the morning the self enters not only into the physical body but into the terrestrial forces altogether. It is the self which places itself within the forces in the act of standing up. A purely spiritual entity, the self acts directly on a physical force – and this is magic. It is the same with every movement of our limbs, of our whole body: they are magical deeds.

This magic is, however, limited and kept within the boundary of our skin. It was not always so. At the time of the ancient continent of Lemuria, man's will-forces could work on the fire element in nature and, through it, could change his physical environment. It was the misuse of these powers that brought about the destruction of Lemuria. Then followed the age of Atlantis when man was still capable of working with his will-forces on the element of water and, by these means, on the life-processes in plants, animals and human beings. As the misuse of fire-magic had destroyed Lemuria so the misuse of water-magic brought the flood that destroyed Atlantis.

A certain kind of magic (beyond the natural magic of our body movements) exists even in the post-Atlantean epoch in which we live. This magic works through the element air and affects human souls. It is the magic of words. It is used in a good sense in church rituals such as the Mass or the Act of Consecration of Man. Any genuine ritual is an act of word-magic.

The Jews of ancient times were forbidden to speak aloud the name of God, Yahweh. Only the High Priest on the Day of Atonement was allowed to utter the sacred word. And if any ordinary man had pronounced this word he would have become insane, as Rudolf Steiner told the workmen in a lecture (Nine Lectures on Bees, Oct 8, 1923). This too belongs to the realm of word-magic. And so does the power of mantric meditations, of which Rudolf Steiner has given so many. But all true poets – and all demagogues – have always known that there is magic in words.

If we now recapitulate the three forms of magic: fire magic working on the physical plane, water magic influencing etheric processes, air magic (or word magic) affecting the astral body, we can see what the next stage of magic will have to be: earth magic which affects the I or self. And there is only one place where the self and the earth-forces come together: the human physical body. And what was quoted at the beginning, Rudolf Steiner's remarks about the magical activity of the I when we make any physical movement, gives already the direction of the magic which is to come.

There is a special name for this kind of magic – the magic of the Holy Grail. What the Grail legend places before us in powerful imaginations is the power which will enable the self to master and to transform the earth element of the body. We discussed the Grail magic already in connection with the two pillars, Jachim and Boaz (Chapter 9). It is the magic by means of which man will be able to do consciously for himself what at present the plants do unconsciously for him; the photosynthesis that divides carbon dioxide into carbon and oxygen.

But the coming of the magic of the Grail also and inevitably brings the arch-enemy of the Grail, the Antichrist, who is the supreme master of all black magic. He too wants to get hold of the esoteric forces of the human physical body, but by means of destroying this body. This is the reason why the worst form of black magic has the aim of inflicting painful death on other human beings. The Antichrist and his servants gain occult powers from the destruction of living human bodies.

Rudolf Steiner gave a picture of such black magic practices (Inner Impulses of Evolution, Sep 24, 1916). He spoke about the mysteries of ancient Mexico. These mysteries were founded on human sacrifices. Every year thousands of victims were killed on the altars of those temples by having their hearts ripped out of their living bodies. The lecture goes on to tell of a priest who had performed such sacrifices through many incarnations and had by this means gained so much occult power that the spiritual world, the good gods, had to intervene. At the time of the Mystery of Golgotha a hero, the protagonist of the good powers, overpowered the black magician and had him crucified. Through the crucifixion the evil power was broken and destroyed forever.

What is remarkable in this story is the power of the cross. For the Romans the cross was the symbol of a shameful death; for Christianity it is the sign of salvation. But the Mexican story reveals the occult power inherent in the simple form of the cross. Not any kind of death, but death on the cross destroyed the power of the Mexican priest.

There is indeed a good magic force connected with the form of the cross and this is the reason why making the sign of the cross is an essential part of any Christian service. And the legends that assert that the devil flees when someone crosses himself show that there existed an instinctive knowledge of the power of the cross. This knowledge is even older than Christianity, as can be seen in the Egyptian cross symbol which appears in so many pictures of gods and kings.

The cross is simply by its form a centre of spiritual forces. It is a very abstract form but, as such, it is an extract of the formative forces that build the human body. The reality of these forces is the cross formed by the four animals shown on the second seal: the Eagle, the Bull, the Lion and Man. These images are meant to convey the cosmic regions where the main forces that form the body originate: the constellations of the zodiac of Scorpio (also called Eagle), Taurus, Leo, and Aquarius. And these constellations too form a cross. These four are also spoken of in the Apocalypse and it is said that they behold God in eternity and praise him (Rev.4:7f). And this can lead us to an understanding of the source of the power of the cross: it is the Father God, exalted above all beings. And the human body is his work.

What is so special about this body, frail and mortal as it is? The human body is on the one hand as physical as any stone or piece of wood. It is on the other hand so spiritual that a pure spirit, the I, can be present in it and be united with it. And in Christ's Resurrection his human body was completely spiritualised. The human body is physical and spiritual at the same time. This is, however, also the nature of the Father God of whom it is said in the Creed of the Christian Community: 'an almighty divine being, spiritual-physical ... goes before his creatures like a Father.' This is what the four beasts 'praise' – that means what they reveal in their harmony: a body that is yet spirit. And the extract of this harmony is the cross.

Because the human body is both a physical and a spiritual entity it is also the bearer of magical forces, since magic consists, as was explained earlier, in producing physical effects by spiritual means or, as in the case of the Mexican mysteries, spiritual effects by physical means. The human body is the bearer of the most ancient archetypal magic, the magic of the Father God. This is the magic that the Antichrist seeks to make his own by the violation and destruction of the human body. This is why black magic leads to the slaughter of innocent victims, as in the case of Gilles de Rais (a contemporary of Joan of Arc) who had killed hundreds of children before his misdeeds were discovered; as in the case of the Marquis de Sade whose 'sadistic' fantasies inspired several mass-murderers, right up to the present; or as in the case of the professional torturers who are a product of more recent times. Such phenomena are an indication that souls who once belonged to the Mexican mystery stream are incarnated in Europe in order to prepare for the coming of their master, the two-horned beast.

And just as in the Jewish tradition the name of God was too sacred to be spoken, so John, the writer of the Apocalypse, regards the Hebrew name of the Antichrist to be so fraught with evil that he does not write it down but only hints at the demon's name in such an obscure fashion that no-one but Rudolf Steiner could solve the riddle. John, an initiate of word magic (after all it was he who had written 'In the beginning was the Word'), was keenly aware that the sound of the name could bring the presence of the demon. However, in the age of the consciousness-soul the secrets of this name have to be revealed. And the second seal, of which we have spoken before, the seal with the archetypal animals, contains also the name of the spirit of abomination.

In order to read the esoteric script of the second seal we have to remember that in eurythmy each consonant is connected with one of the signs of the zodiac. The Eagle (or Scorpio) corresponds to S, the Bull to R, the Man (or Aquarius) to M and the Lion to T. The Lamb (or Aries) in the middle corresponds to W. We have also to consider that in Hebrew only consonants are written, not vowels – with one exception: the Hebrew letter for W is also used for U and O. if we now look at the second seal as a secret script it appears like this.

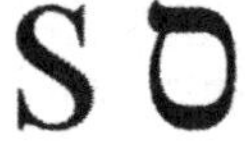

The script of the second seal.

We start with the S, then go to the middle O, then go to the R, then we interpolate the vowel A, (which is not written in Hebrew) and go across to T. The name is SORAT. And what is significant in this word is that M, the consonant for Man is left out. It is an inhuman, anti-human power that is revealed by its name. The second seal, which spoke first to us of the mysteries of the human body, has also now told us the name of the Enemy of Man.

Originally the letters of the name Sorat were written in the Hebrew script and in that ancient script (as also in ancient Greek) the letters of the alphabet stand also for numbers. It is as if we used the letter A for 1, B for 2 and so on. And if we take the Hebrew letters of the evil name as numerals they total

666. This is the reason why John writes in the Apocalypse, 'the number of the beast is six hundred and sixty-six.' It is his way of indicating the word without writing it.

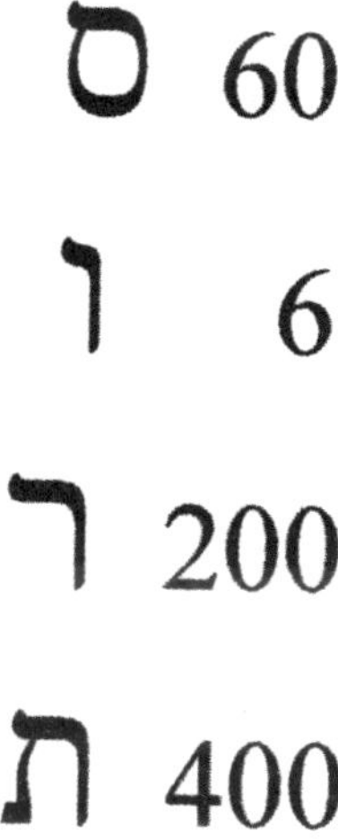

The Hebrew letters and their numbers

Yet the number 666 has a meaning. There are seven stages of evolution from Saturn to Vulcan, each divided into seven sub-stages and each of these is again divided into seven shorter periods. The sixth stage in each of these sequences is the one before the final one. This penultimate stage is the stage of judgment. It is the moment when it will be decided which souls can go on to the final reunion and which cannot. And the souls that have chosen Sorat as their master will not be allowed to go on to the final 777 – they remain with Sorat at 666.

Even the period of 666 years is of evil omen. In the year 666 the anti-Christian philosophy of the Academy of Gondishapur (in Persia) made its assault on Europe. The Arabs, fired by the teaching of Muhammad, would have imposed this philosophy on the still dreaming souls of the peoples of Europe if they had not been defeated by Charles Martel, the grandfather of Charlemagne. In 1332 (2 x 666) it was the Pope and the King of France who liquidated the order of the Knights Templar and so destroyed the esoteric Christianity that was the secret of this order.

The year 1998 (3 x 666) marked the end of the twentieth century and once again the forces of evil, the forces of 666, were let loose on the world. The signs of the increasing influence of that power in our time become more obvious; that power which, unlike Lucifer and Ahriman, cannot and will not be redeemed; the ultimate evil.

The German poet Novalis (Rudolf Steiner called him the herald of the Christ Impulse) spoke of 'magical idealism,' of the magic power of ideals. This magical idealism is the weapon the gods have given man to defeat the magic of Sorat.

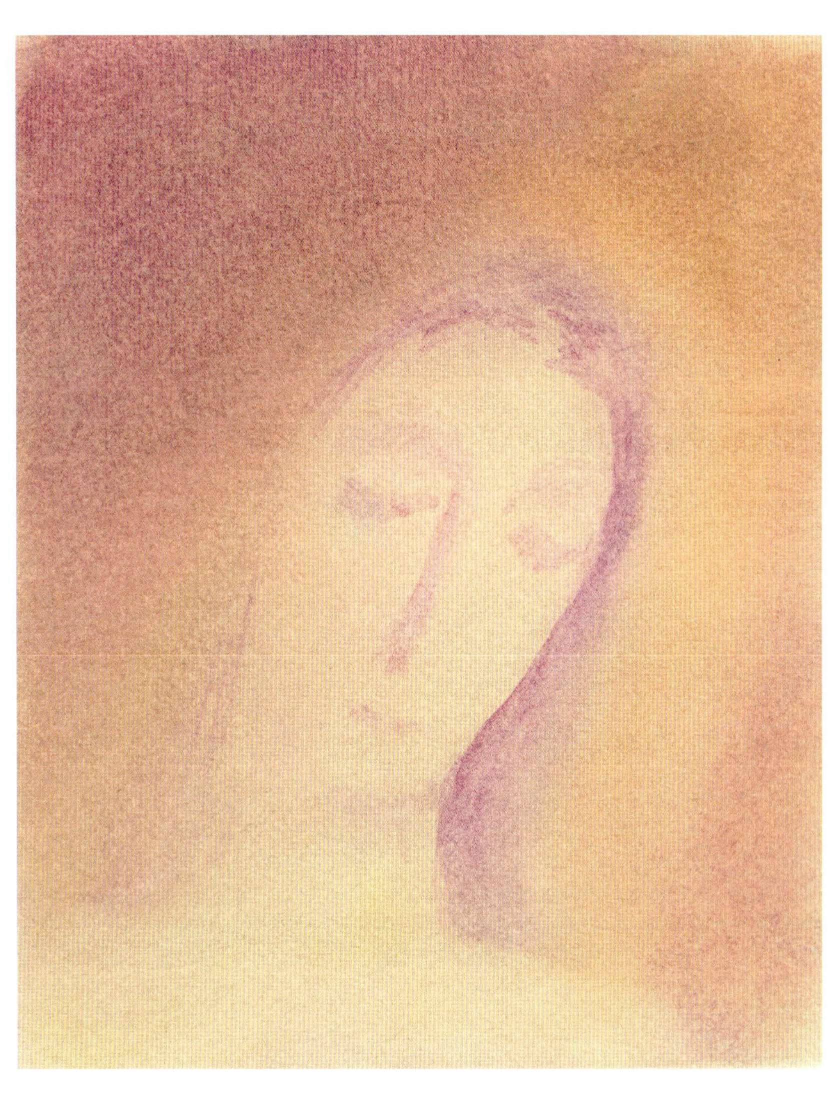

Lazarus-John

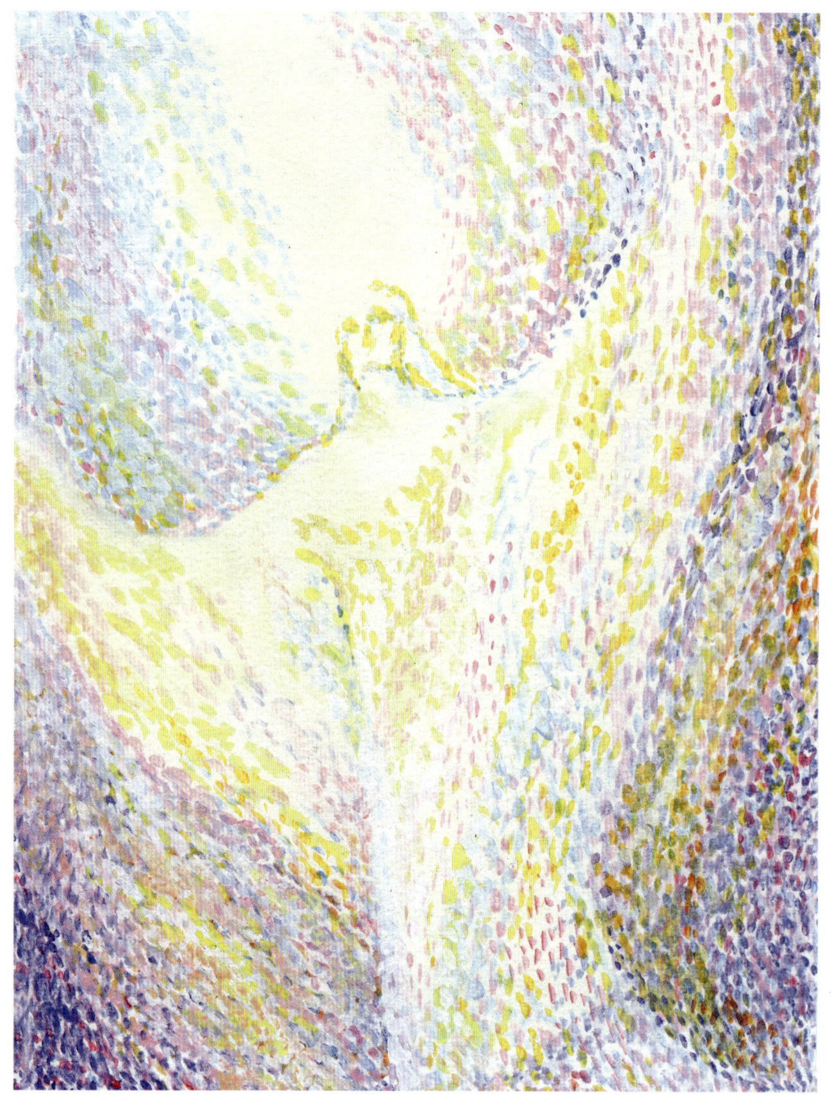

Angel Weaving in the Light

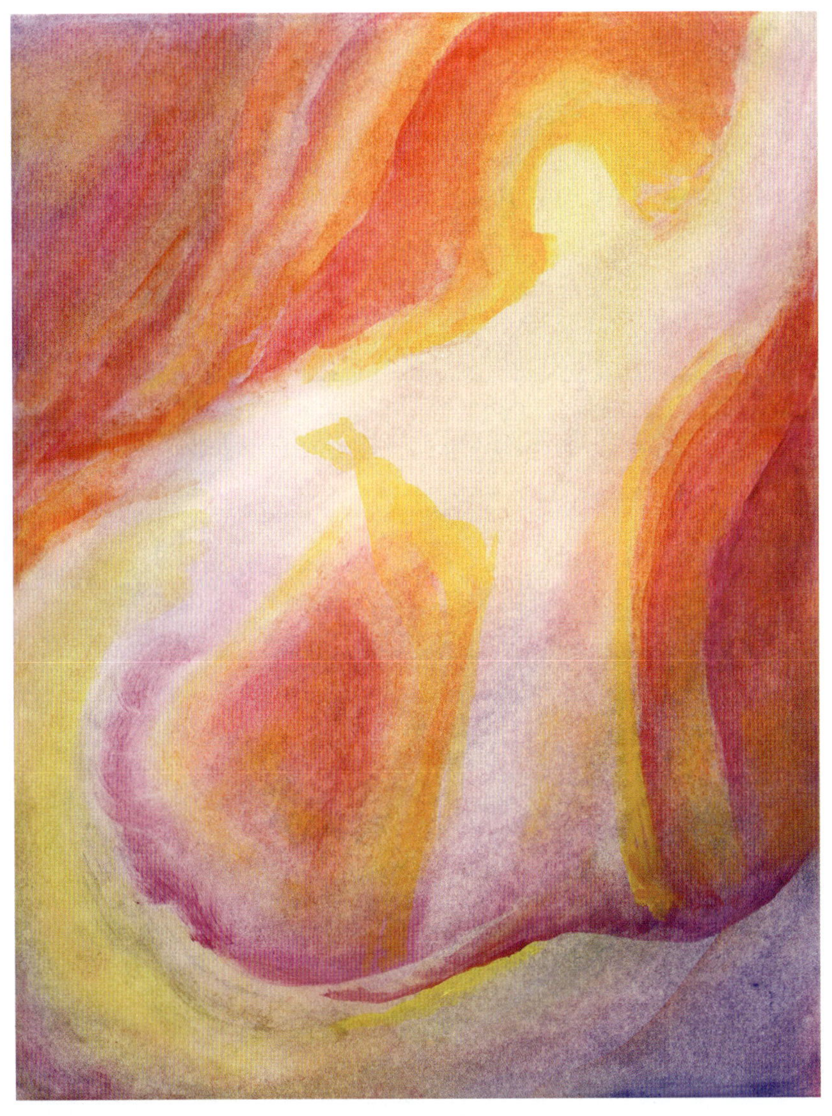

The Archangel Michael

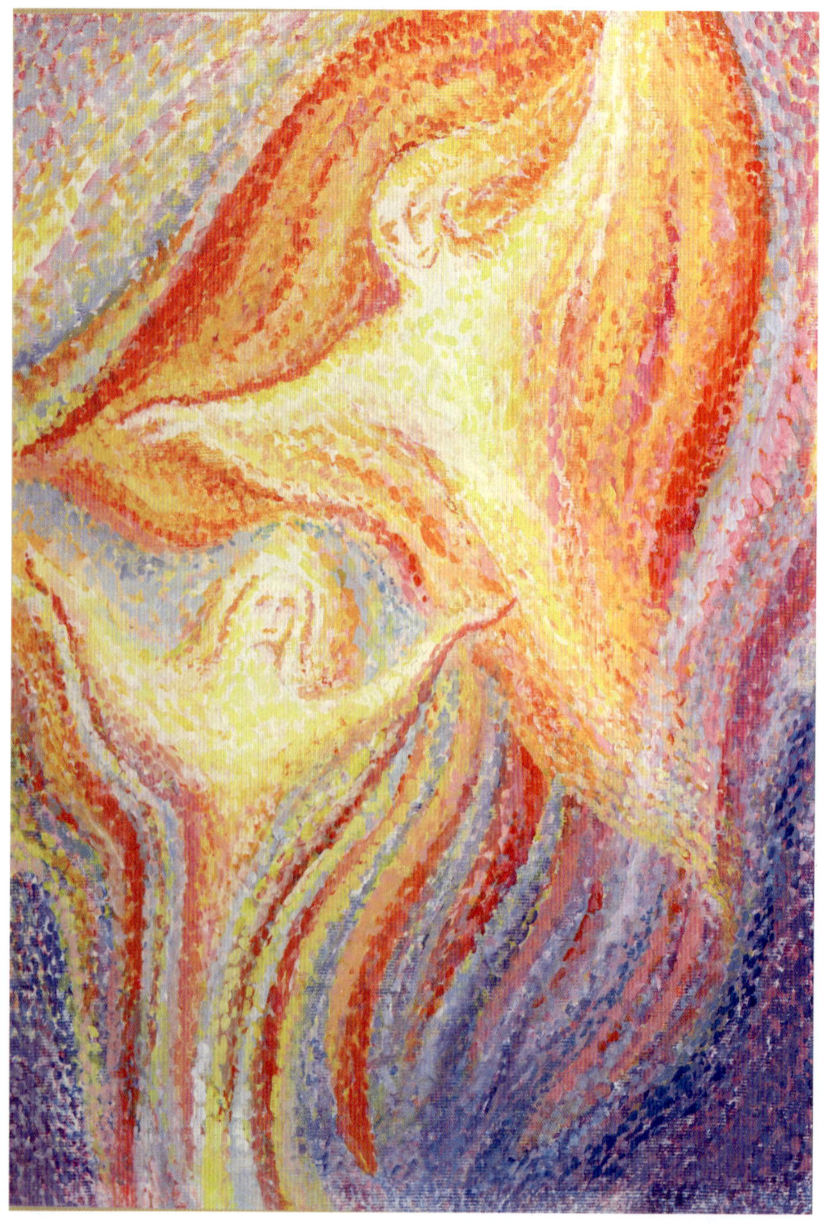

Flower and Sunray

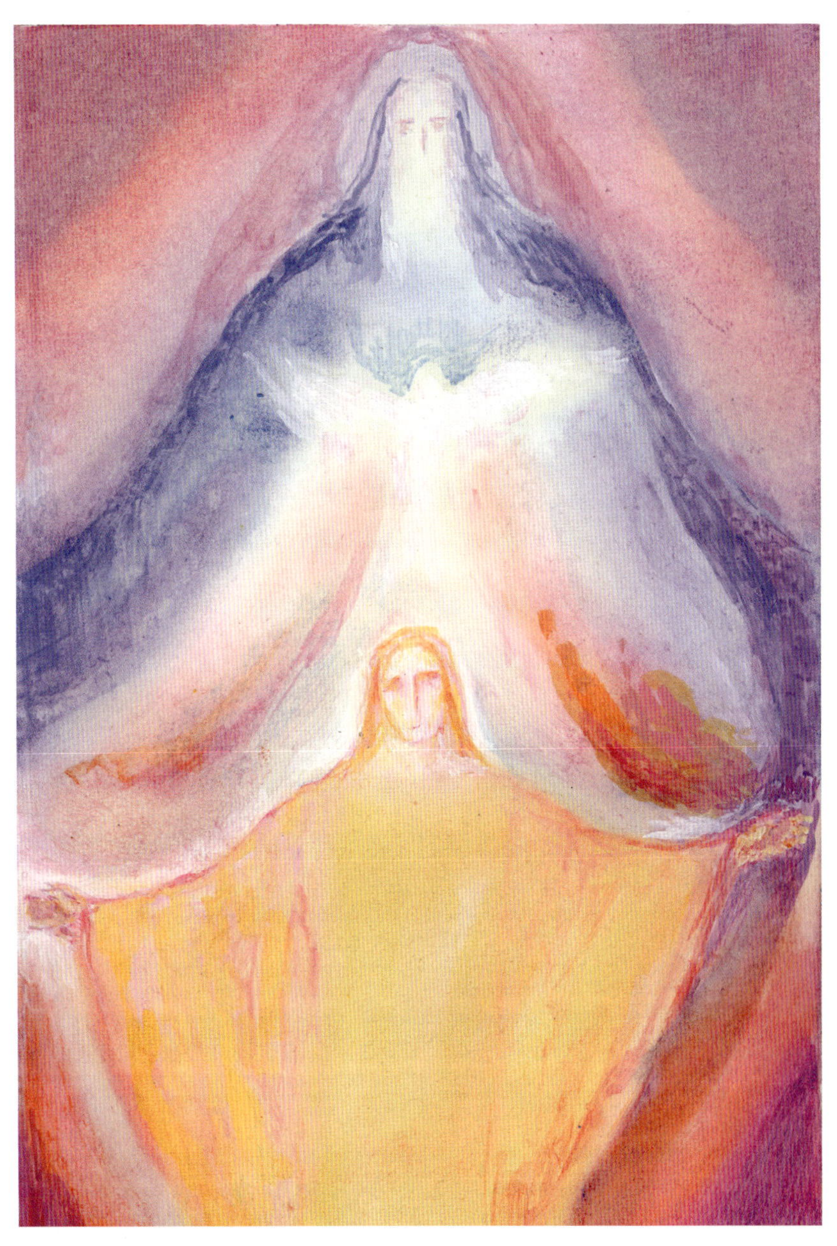

The Trinity

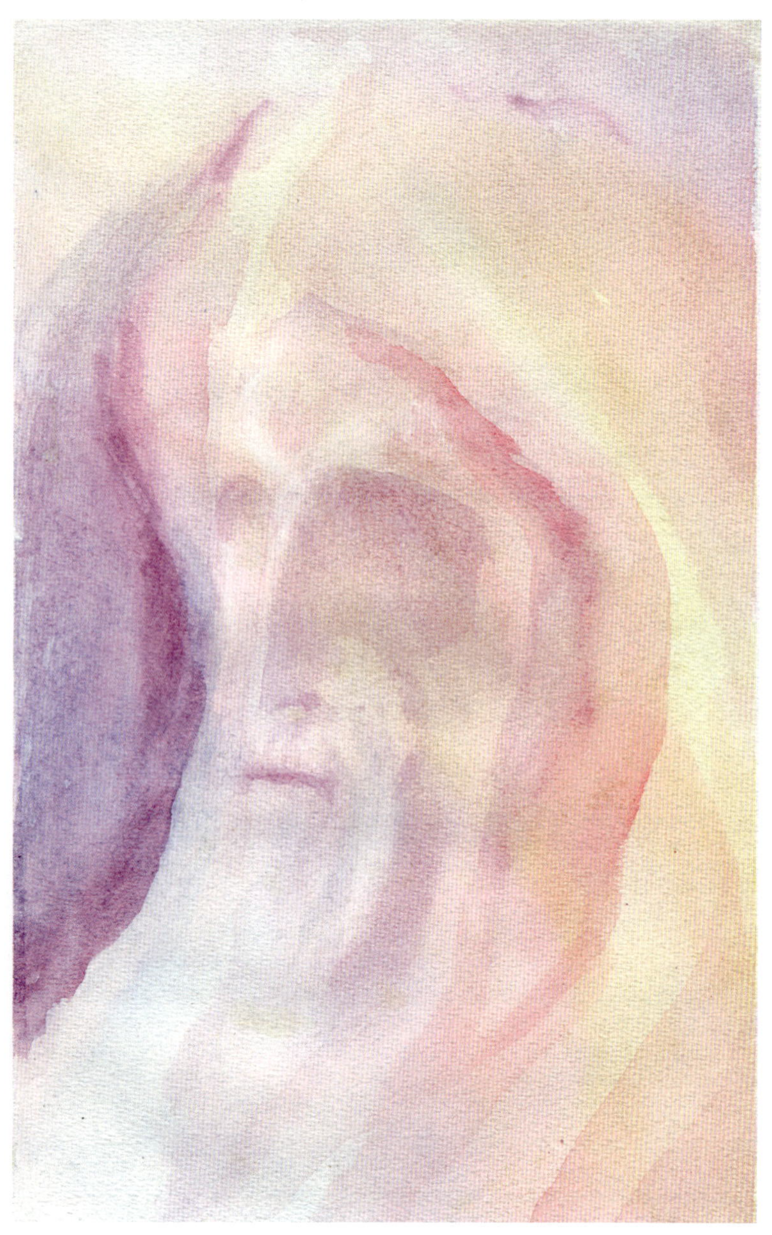

Moses

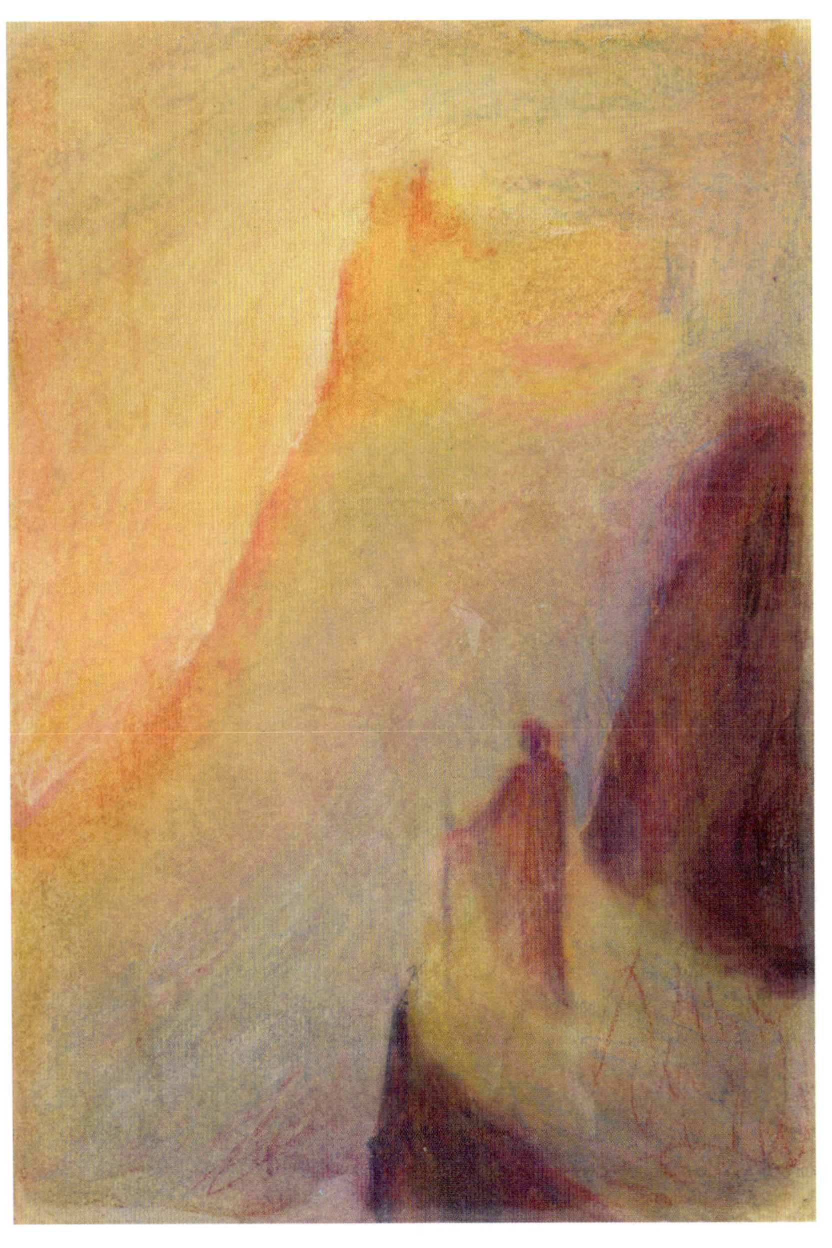

Pilgrim of the Holy Grail

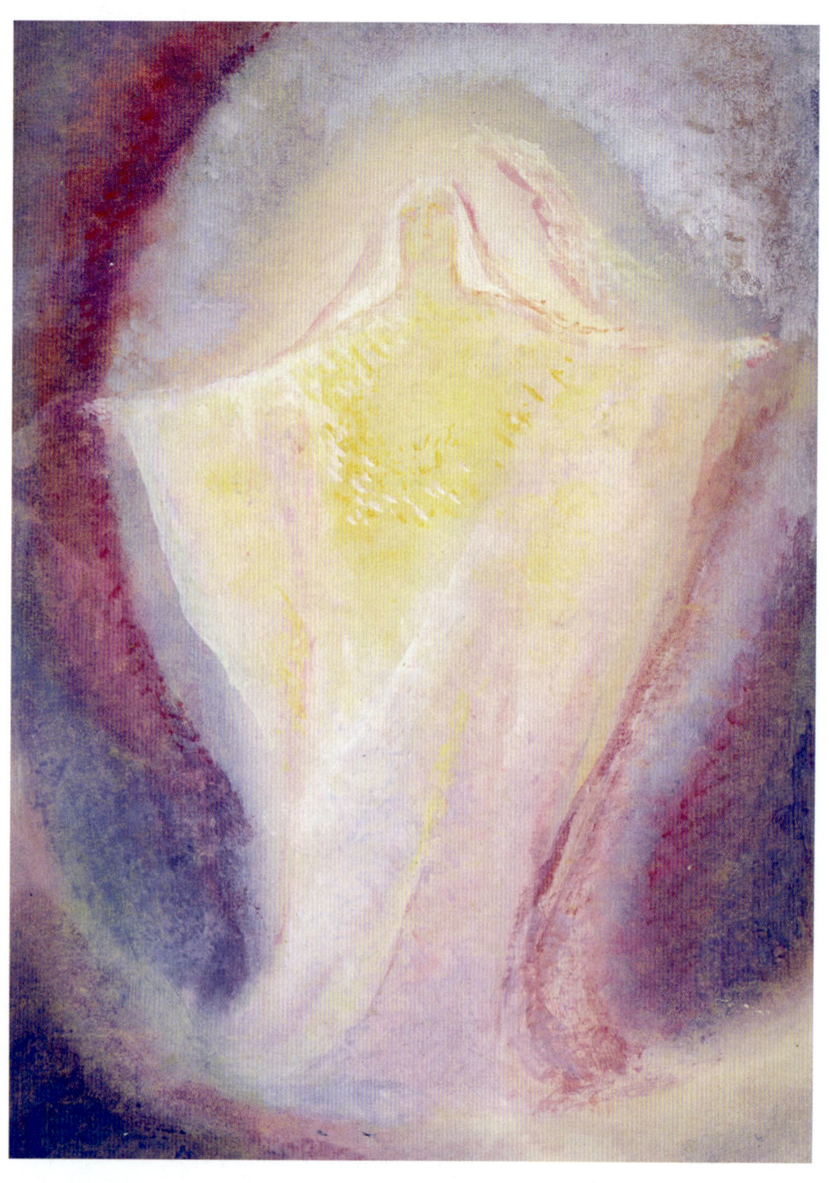

The Woman Standing on the Moon

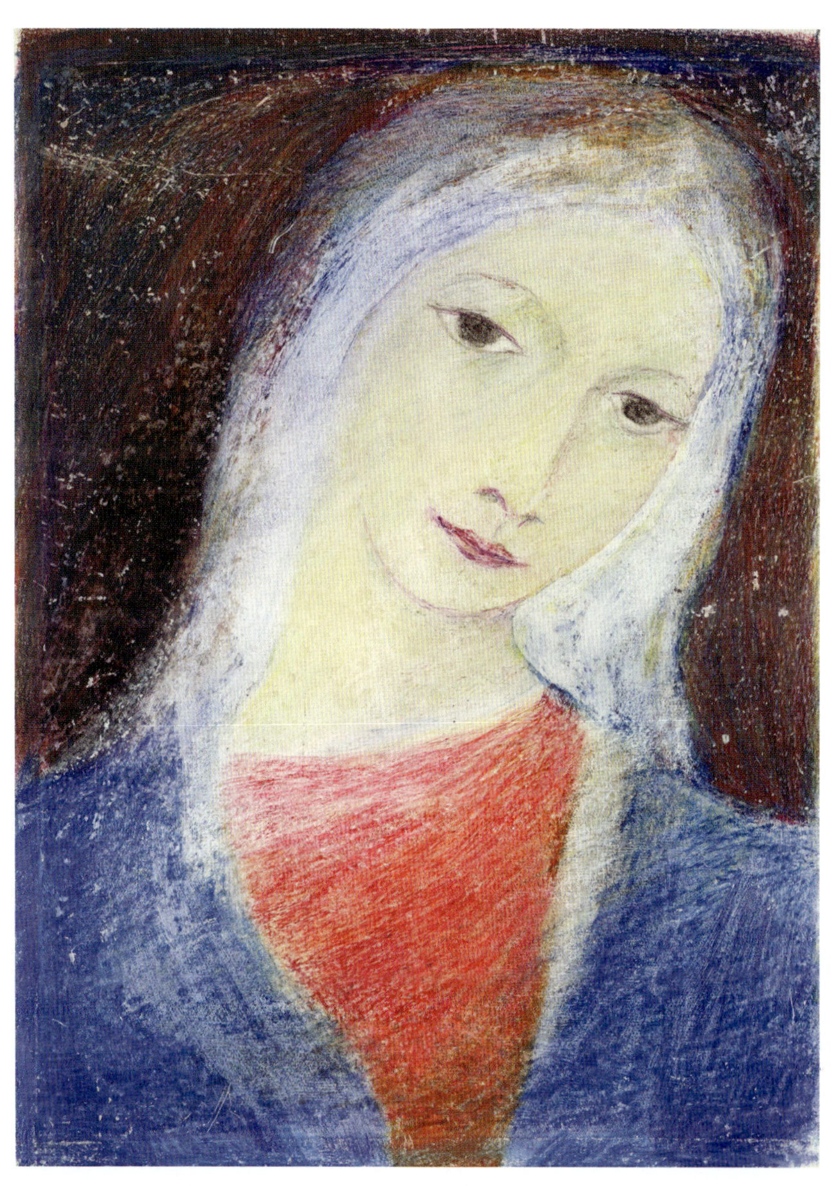

Mary Sophia

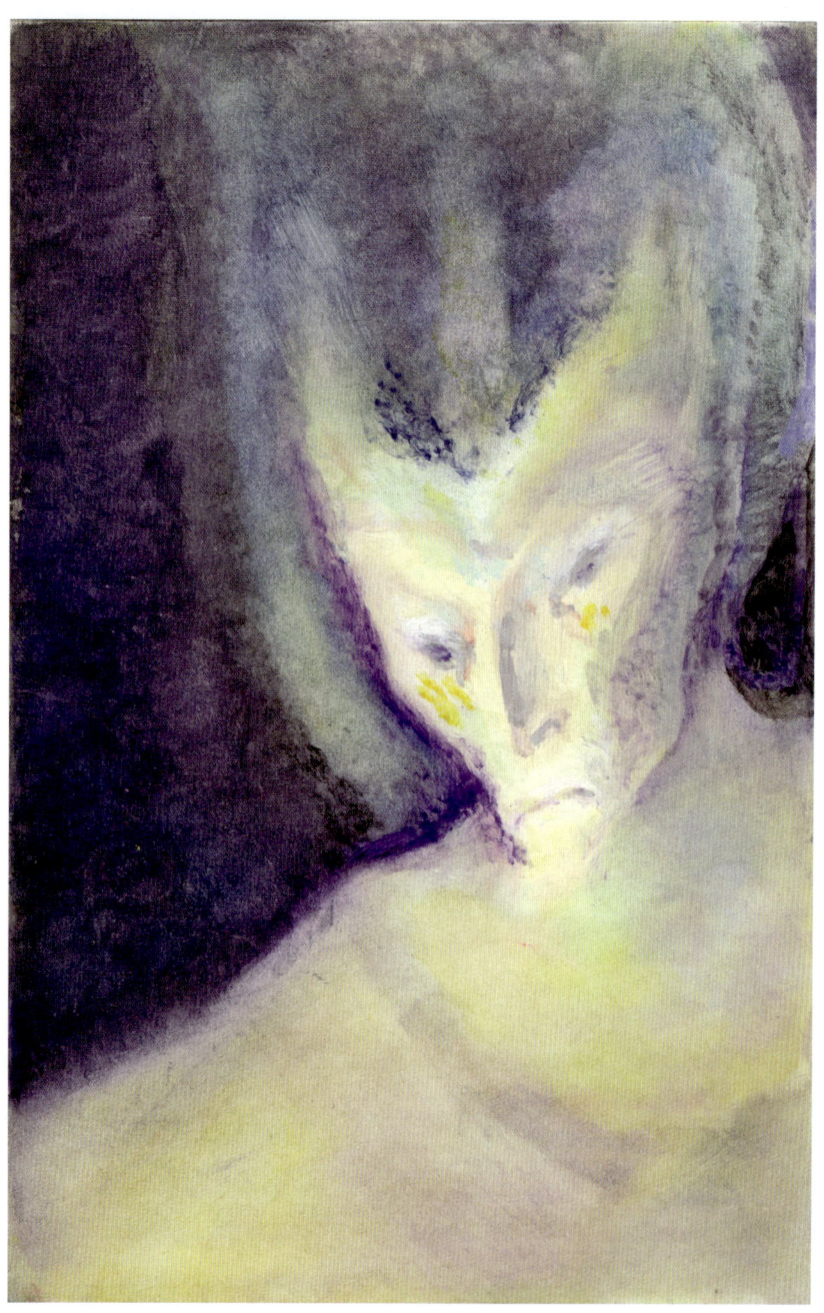

Ahriman

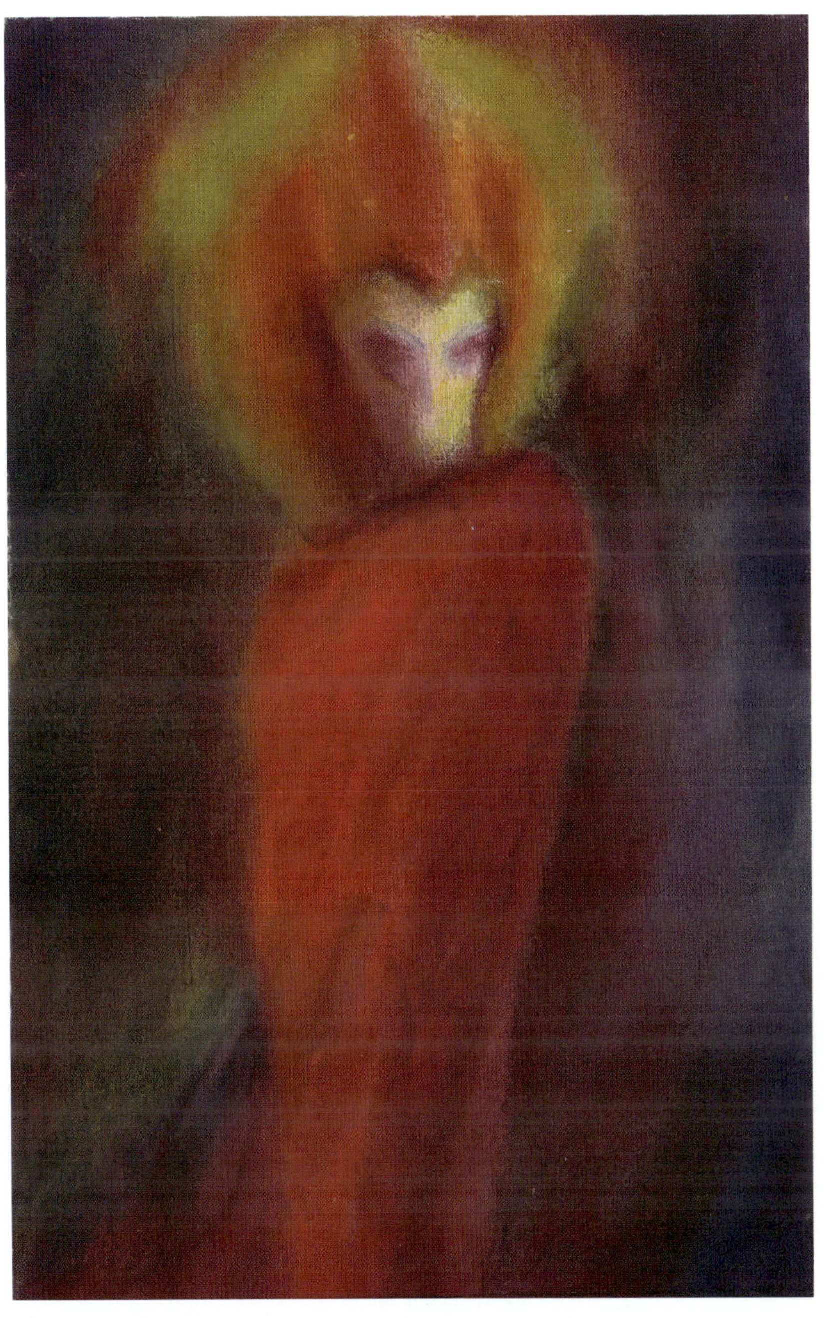

Sorat

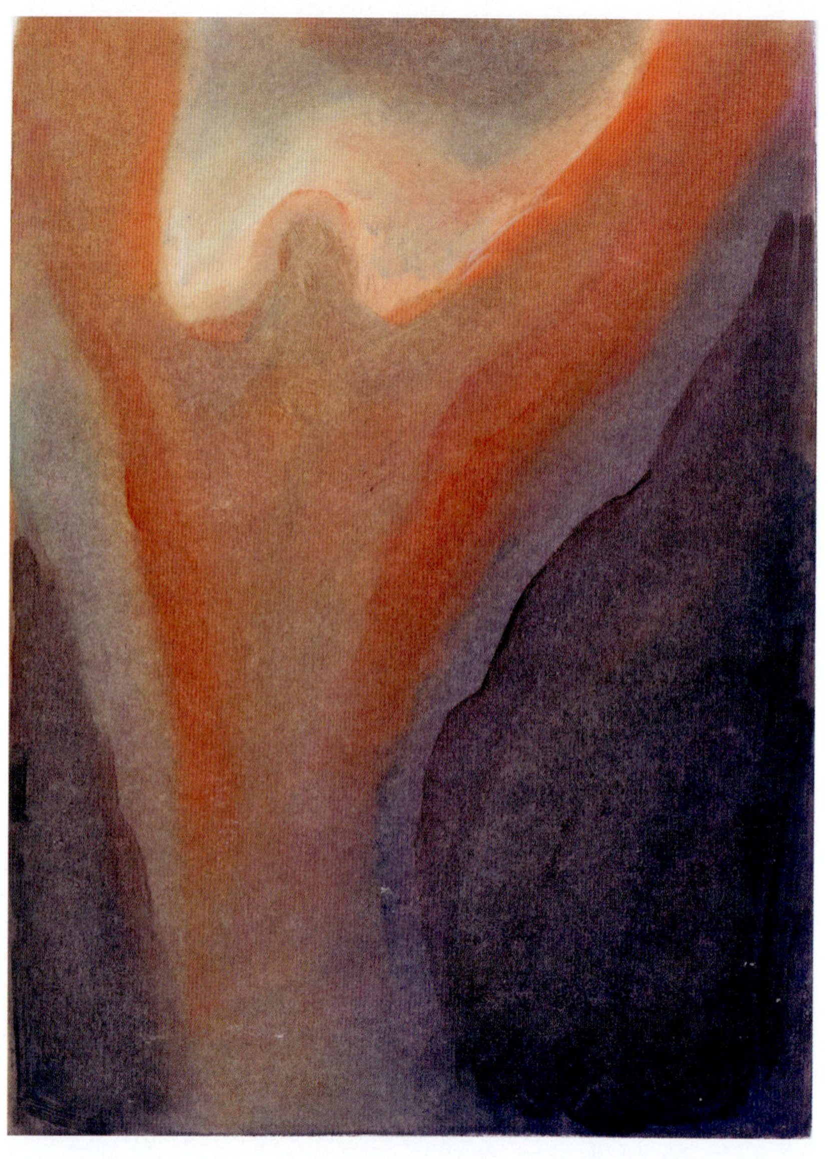

The Angel at the Abyss

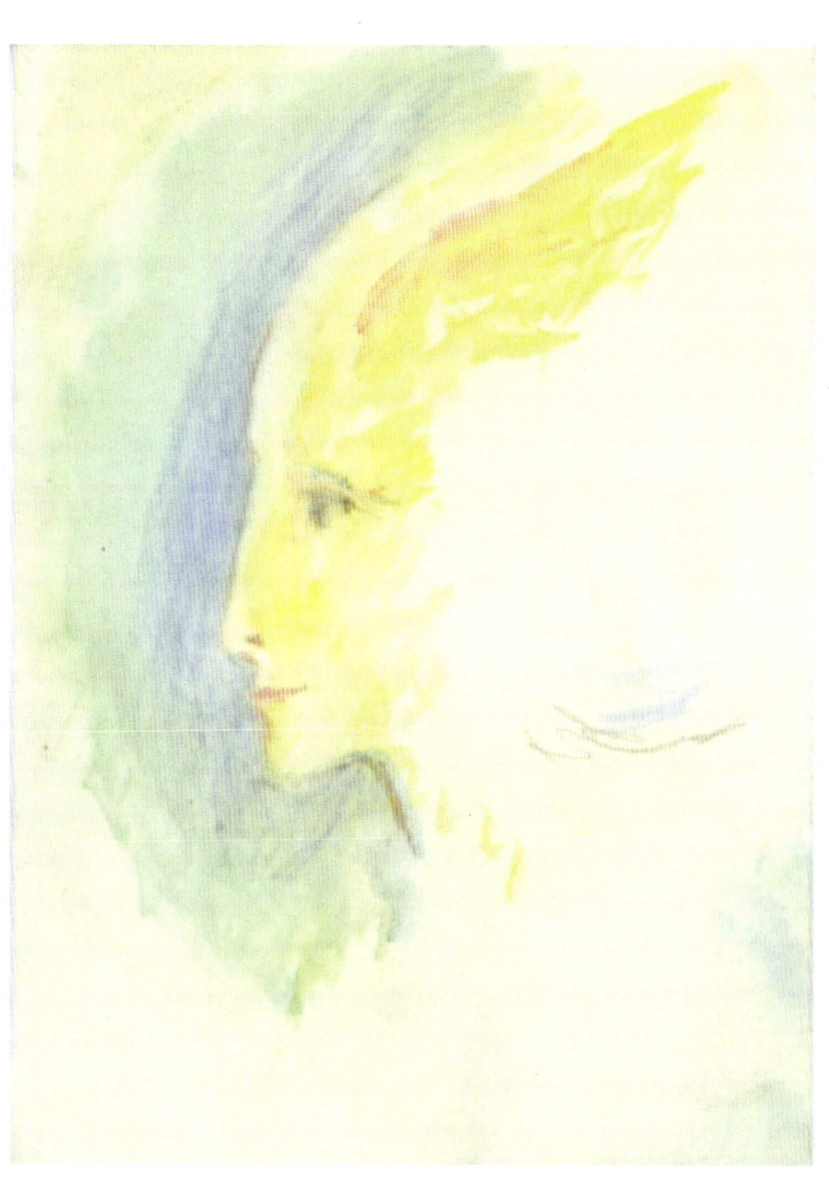

Mercury

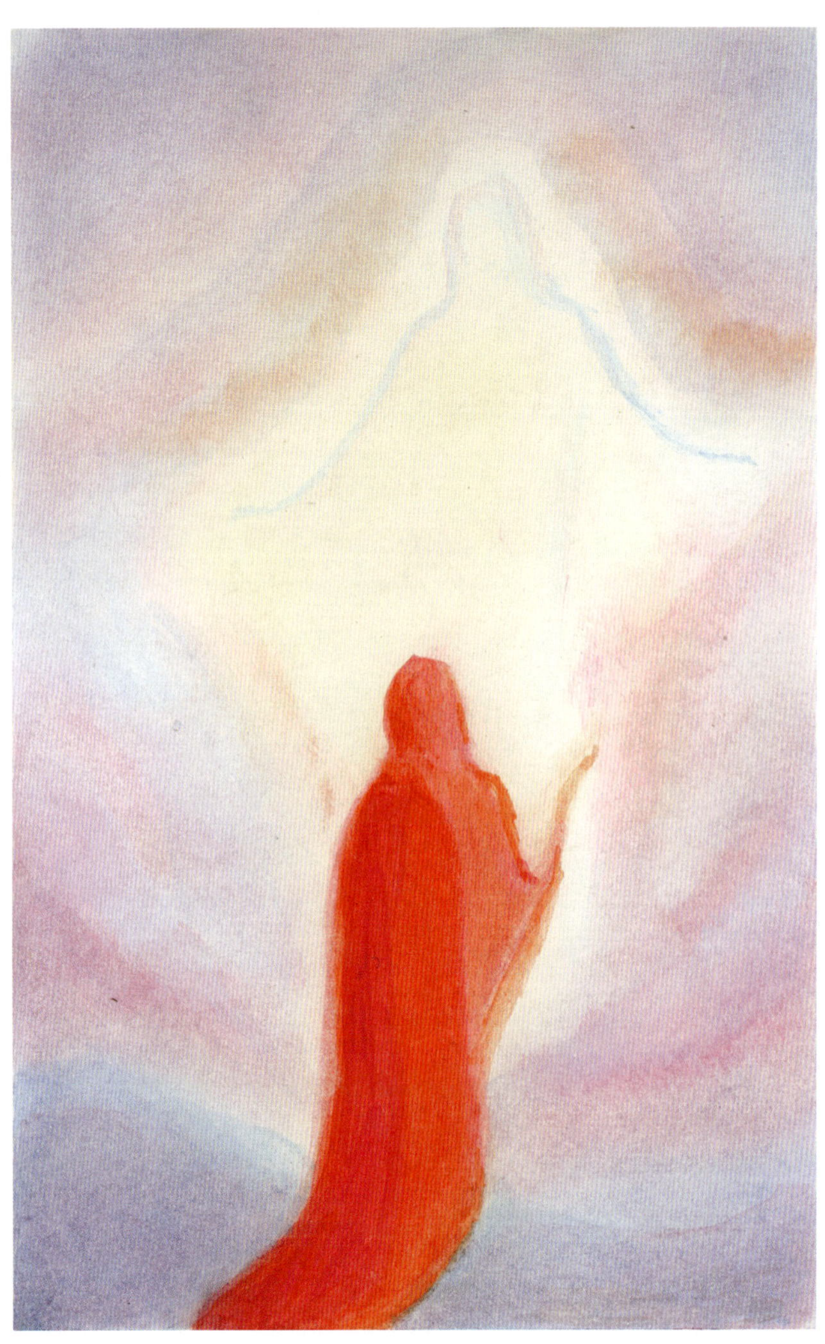

Christ and Mary Magdalene

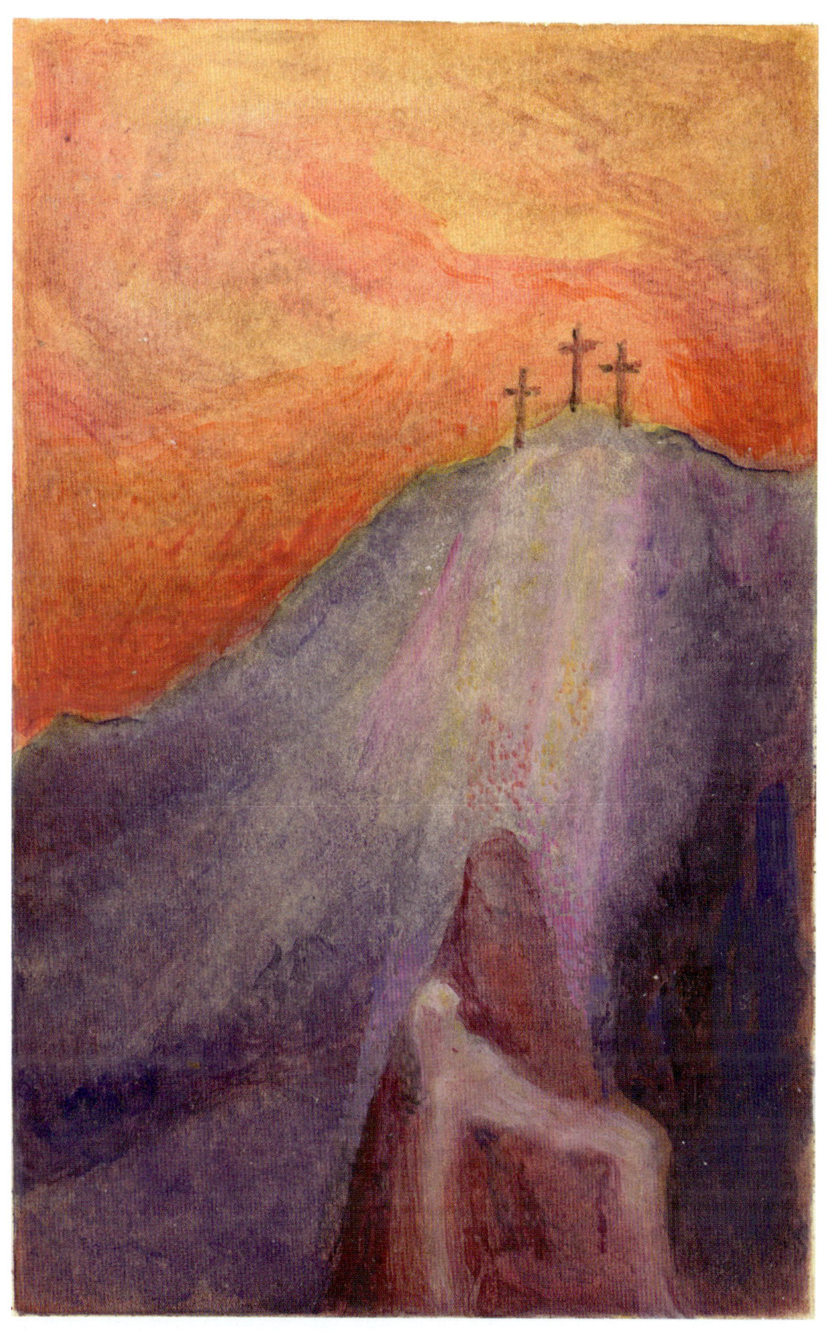

Golgotha

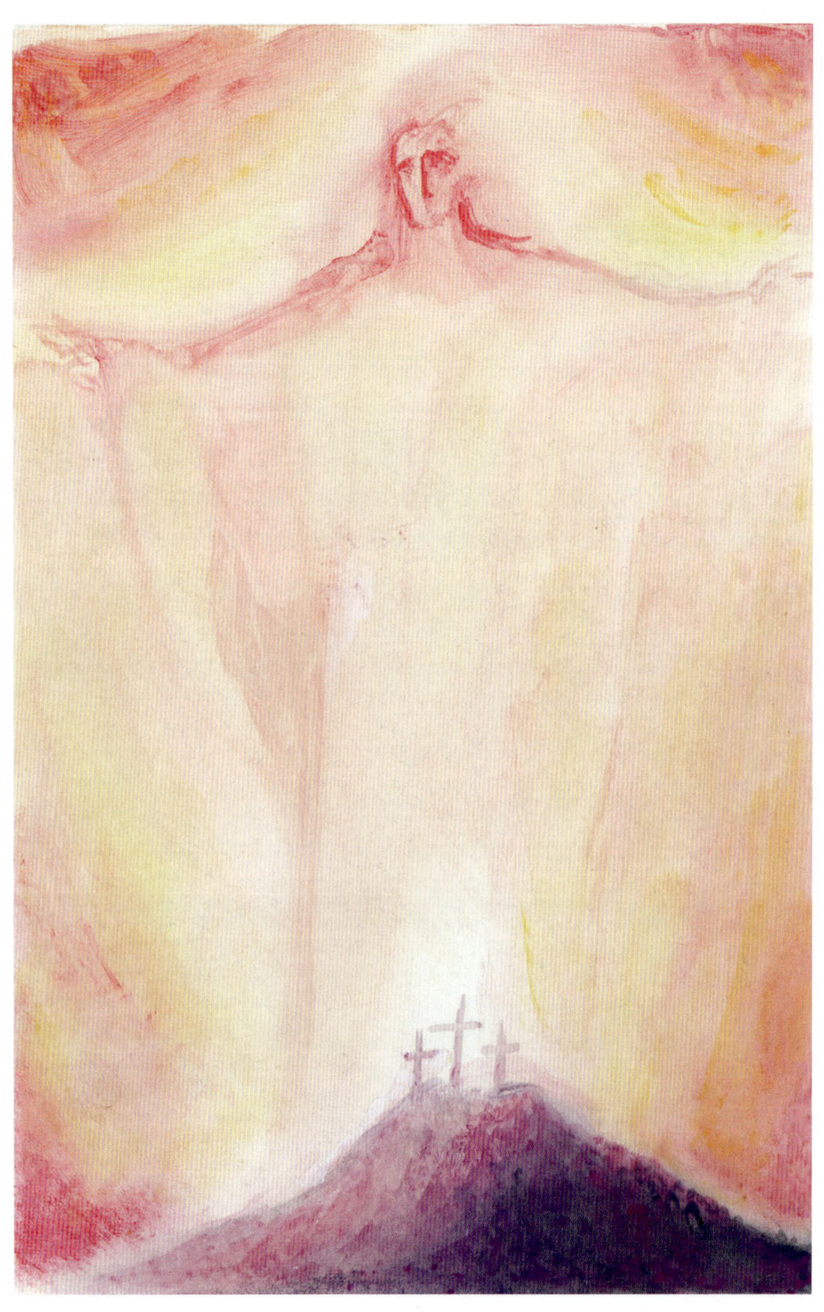

Christ over Golgotha

12

The Woman Who Stands
on the Moon

In the life of the plant the blossom is a metamorphosis or transformation of the green leaf. What can be observed on a small scale in the growth of a flower, the law of transformation, works on a vast scale in the evolution of the world. In a previous stage of Earth evolution, on the Ancient Moon, man was endowed with the astral body; in the next, future stage, on Jupiter, the astral body is to be transformed and will become manas or spirit-self. This is the meaning of the fifth seal, the woman who stands on the moon and bears the sun within her. However, although the manas development will only be completed in the distant future of the Jupiter evolution, it begins already on the present Earth and we are involved in it.

What is meant by transforming the astral body into manas or spirit-self? The animals, too, have astral bodies and the wisdom of the animal instincts has its source in their astral forces. But the astrality of the animals is directed by the group-souls of each species. In man this guidance should be provided by the ego but, as a consequence of the Luciferic temptation and the Fall, the human astral body is not under the tutelage of the self. And when people give way to the instincts and urges of the astral body they can sink lower than the animals. Religious laws such as the Ten Commandments and secular laws upheld by the authority of government have throughout history held human astrality in check, not always very successfully.

But there has also been another way. It is the path of asceticism. By rigorous self-discipline, by self-denial of every kind, by celibate lives and long periods of fasting, men and women of all races have striven to subdue the animal astrality that is present in every one of us. The lives of medieval saints demonstrate the intensity and devotion with which these people pursued the aim of purifying the astral body. Modern man – so satisfied with himself as he is – can have no comprehension of the titanic struggles that took place in the past when souls fought against the fallen nature of the astral body. But was the path of asceticism the right way to rid the soul of passions and desires? Is it really man's task to get rid of them? An answer to these questions was given by Rudolf Steiner in a lecture for members of the Esoteric School (Esoteric Lessons, Aug 27, 1909).

The lecture contains a description of the initiation of Parsifal, which means the real person who stands behind the poetic fiction of the Parsifal saga. This real Parsifal had for a long time lived a life of extreme ascetic discipline and had purified his soul from all low desires. His spiritual development enabled him to raise himself to higher worlds. From there he could in full consciousness look back upon his own being, which was shown to him in the form of an imagination, and what he saw was a big plant from which grew a beautiful flower, a white lily. But this lily – the image of his purified astrality – was surrounded by a horrible stench. Why was there an evil smell? He had expelled passions and desires from his soul but they still existed, unredeemed and unchanged, as astral realities around him. And he heard a voice that said, 'This is what you are.' Then all went dark around Parsifal. After some time another picture appeared before his spiritual vision. It was a black cross intertwined with red roses. But now the bad smell had disappeared, it had been taken away by the roses, and there was only their sweet scent. Again the voice spoke and it said, 'This is what you shall become.'

This was the beginning of Parsifal's initiation. The further stages of this initiation as described in the lecture do not concern us in the present context. What does matter is the juxtaposition of the lily and the rose as symbols for the path of asceticism and the new Rosicrucian path, which is not based on the rejection of desires but on their transformation. The black cross is the symbol for these desires. This is also the meaning of the black cross in the meditation given in Rudolf Steiner's Esoteric Science. In that meditation the roses are to grow from the black cross.

Man is not meant to rid himself of desires but to redeem the forces hidden in them. The power to bring about such a transformation is given to man by the Mystery of Golgotha. In pre-Christian times all forms of initiation stood under the sign of the lily, the symbol of the striving for purity. What was impure in the soul had to be cast out – but was not ennobled. And this pre-Christian principle still guided the monks and nuns of the Christian era for many centuries; it is still accepted by the Church of Rome. The Parsifal initiation that took place in the ninth century marks the transition from the path of the lily to the path that is represented by the cross and the roses.

The symbol of the cross and the roses was not known to many people, but the idea it represented was brought to everyone, to the simplest minds, to children, in the form of fairy tales. Most fairy tales of this kind have their origin in the south of France, in Provence, the region where Parsifal lived. The common feature of these tales is that the hero or heroine meets some animal and has to perform some task, after which the creature becomes a beautiful prince or princess who had only been turned into an animal by some evil enchantment. The story of Beauty and the Beast is the best example of such a fairy tale.

What is regarded as our lower nature, our desires and passions, are 'enchanted' beings, condemned to live in us as animal urges until we can restore them to their true nature, which is pure and good. This is the message of these fairy tales. It is also the meaning of the story of the Sleeping Beauty. Here the hedge of thorns represents the dark side of the astral body. The hero has to break through the thorns to find and to awaken the beautiful princess.

What is it that is hidden, unawakened, enchanted in our astral nature? Who is the sleeping princess or the enchanted prince? The answer to this question can be found in the gospels. They tell us of a woman who was brought before Christ so that he should condemn her and her way of life for she was a 'sinner,' which, in the Old Testament sense, meant a prostitute. But instead of expressing any condemnation or reproach Christ says, 'her sins, which are many, are forgiven, for she loved much' (Luke 7:47). This sinful woman is the one who became Mary Magdalene. It is not an accident that she was the first to see the Lord after the Resurrection.

What lived in the desires that had made her a prostitute and what was awakened and redeemed by Christ was the power of love. But it is the same with all our desires; all desiring is loving something. Through Lucifer this love element has been reduced to a lower level. He is the enchanter who cast the spell upon man's astral body. Through him the love element is hidden in desires that were in their rightful place on the Ancient Moon when the human being was still at the animal stage.

In as far as we are capable of freeing love from the spell of the Luciferic forces, we awaken in us the 'sleeping beauty' that is manas or spirit-self. Selfless love is the magic that breaks the spell of Lucifer. And the Greek word St Paul used for love, agapé, does not mean 'charity' as the Authorised Version sometimes has it; it means love that is free from desire (1Cor.13:4). And what the Apocalypse wants to convey by the image of the woman, who has the Moon under her feet and brings forth a Sun from her heart, is this transformation of desire into agapé.

However, there are powers (of a Luciferic nature) whose aim is to prevent this transformation. The Apocalypse presents these adversary powers in the image of the Whore of Babylon. There is a reason for using the name Babylon in this context. In the Babylonian civilisation there existed the institution of hierodules. They were priestesses of the goddess of love, Astarte, and they gave themselves to men in honour of their goddess. This is the origin of prostitution, the sin of Mary Magdalene. It was, to begin with, a religious practice performed in the service of the goddess Astarte, the Babylonian counterpart to the Roman Venus. For the writer of the Apocalypse, Babylon, with its cult of Astarte, became thus the symbol for the spirits who want to keep man at the animal stage of the Ancient Moon.

There is a German saga in which all the themes that have been mentioned in connection with the fifth seal are interwoven. It is the story of Tannhäuser, which inspired Wagner to write one of his great operas. The saga speaks of a mountain where, deep inside, the goddess Venus (or Astarte) still held sway as she did in ancient times. It was a region shunned by all good Christians, but a troubadour, a poet and singer named Tannhäuser, found his way into the hidden kingdom of Venus and stayed there for a long time.

Eventually he tore himself away from Venus and returned to the world in order to take part in a contest of troubadours which, incidentally, was an historical event. At the Wartburg (the castle where the contest took place) he could only sing of physical, sensual love; he did not know any other. But another contestant there was Wolfram von Eschenbach – the poet who wrote the epic of Parsifal and the Holy Grail – and Wolfram sang of another kind of love. His song praised the love whose symbol is the Grail. Tannhäuser was deeply moved by the song; he was gripped by shame and remorse and decided to go on a pilgrimage to Rome to obtain forgiveness for his sojourn in the Venus Mountain from the Pope himself. He met a band of pilgrims on their way to Rome and wanted to join them, but their leader refused him when he heard what Tannhäuser's sin had been. He told him, 'This sin can never be forgiven, no more than the pilgrim's staff you hold can bear blossoms.' Tannhäuser despairs. He drove his staff into the earth and went back to the one place where he would be welcome, the Venus Mountain. He had already left when the pilgrims witness a miracle: from the dead wood of Tannhäuser's staff, red roses were blooming.

The final feature of the legend makes it quite clear that this story, too, came from Rosicrucian sources and contains the message that Parsifal had received in his visions. But there is also something else that this story wants to convey. It is indicated by the nature of Tannhäuser's calling: he is a troubadour, a poet and singer. And so was another mythical figure, Orpheus, the Greek hero whose songs and music tamed wild animals so that they came and lay down peacefully at his feet.

In the Orpheus myth the animals are again symbols of man's astral forces; they are tamed by music – which stands for art in all its forms – music, poetry, painting. The myth expresses the mission of art: it works on the astral forces and gradually subdues their animal nature. Art does for the human soul what we as individuals are mostly too self-indulgent to do: it works in the direction of manas and raises our desire-nature to a higher level. In the love of music, or any other art, there is already something awakening that is higher than the primitive desires. In art, in the enjoyment of art, the gods have given humankind a helper towards the distant goal of manas. And Tannhäuser, because he is a singer and poet like Orpheus, is connected with the manas impulse, whether he knows it or not. That is why the roses grow from his staff even when he is going back to Venus.

Manas or spirit-self is not some abstraction, not some abstract ideal we are supposed to aim for; it is a being that the esoteric schools of the Gnostics called Sophia. This being appeared in a human body as the mother of the Solomonic Jesus, she who stood by the Cross of Golgotha. The Apocalypse describes her cosmic nature in the image of the woman who stands on the moon and brings forth a sun. All true artists are her servants, just as the hierodules of ancient Babylon were the servants of Astarte. And any human soul that can enjoy some form of art is, through this enjoyment, preparing itself for the awakening of manas. This preparation takes place on an unconscious level, in the realm of feeling. There is also a preparation for manas, for Sophia, in full waking consciousness. It is called anthroposophy.

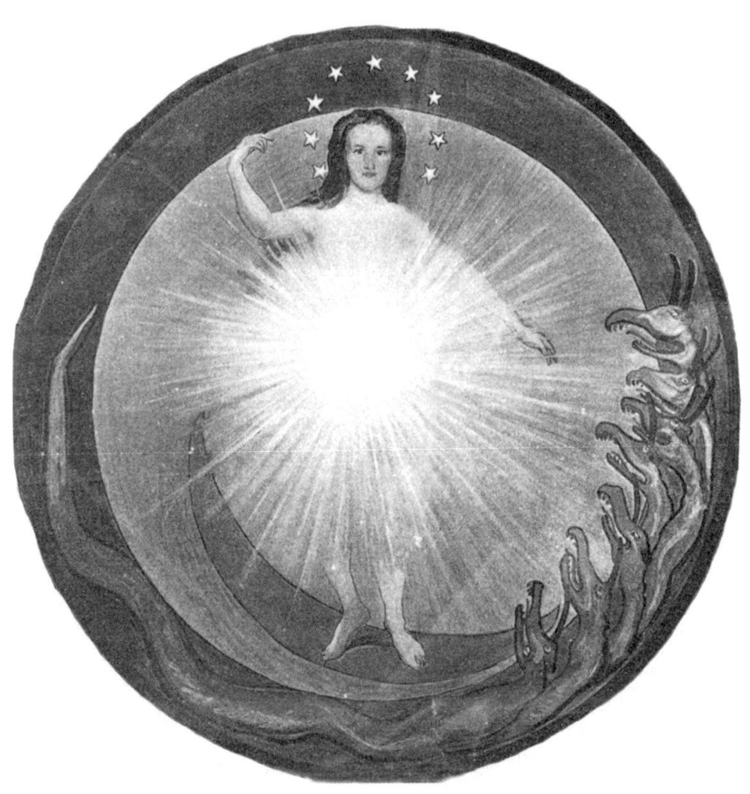

Sketch of the fifth seal of the Apocalypse

13

The Archangel Michael

The imaginations presented in the seven seals have very profound meanings, as we have found in the course of these studies. The main significance of these pictures designed by Rudolf Steiner is, however, that they refer to the seven stages of evolution, from Ancient Saturn to Vulcan as they are described in Esoteric Science. And as the fifth seal, the woman standing on the moon, refers to the fifth stage, the Jupiter evolution, so the sixth seal is meant to express the sixth stage, the Venus evolution. It is the stage in which man will transform the etheric body into buddhi or life-spirit. It may seem surprising that the image chosen for this stage is the familiar motif of Michael and the dragon. What is the connection between Michael and the future task of transforming the etheric body?

To find an answer to this question let us first consider the etheric body as it is at the present Earth stage of evolution. What is the main function of the etheric body? It builds, in the beginning of every earth life, the physical body. Although the 'design' of the human physical body is the work of the highest hierarchies, it is the etheric body which 'imprints' this design on the physical substances from which our body is formed. The etheric body is the bearer of the life-forces which maintain all the functions which are necessary for the body to exist here on earth. When the etheric body is withdrawn at the end of life, the physical body disintegrates; it has no power to preserve its form. The form of the human physical body is not owing to the physical body, but to the etheric body. Yet – as Rudolf

Steiner explained in a lecture, the etheric body could, by its own nature, not give us the human form (Spiritual Science as a Foundation, Sep 4, 1920). It has a strong kinship with the animal world, so much so that if we look at an elephant, our etheric body takes on the elephant shape. The etheric body could form us in the likeness of animals but could not impose on the earthly substances the human form. The astral body is even less capable of doing so since – as is pointed out in the same lecture – it can go no further than the shape of plants. And the I, the 'baby' among the four members of the human organisation, has even less power and is less developed than the astral or the etheric body. So where does the human form we bear during life on earth come from?

Rudolf Steiner revealed that it was Michael who, in the middle of the Lemurian period, when the first human souls incarnated on Earth, gave their bodies the human form. We have therefore to see in Michael the spirit who overcomes the animal tendencies in the etheric body and gives the etheric forces the direction which leads to the development of the form which the gods intended for man from the beginning of the world.

And when in the distant Venus evolution man will transform the etheric body, when the human ego will have to take conscious control of the etheric forces, then the ego will also have to take over the task at present entrusted to Michael: the overcoming of the animal forces. We ourselves will have to become like Michael. The Michael image of the sixth seal is a picture of what we ourselves are to become.

The sixth stage of evolution is for us who are still in the fourth stage, Earth, inconceivably far away. But, as was mentioned on an earlier occasion, the seven great stages of evolution are subdivided into seven shorter periods and each of these periods is again subdivided into seven smaller epochs. And every time we come in these subdivisions to the sixth step, something takes place which is, on a smaller scale, similar in character to the 'Great Six.'

We live now in the fifth post-Atlantean epoch, which will be followed by the sixth. And in that sixth (the Slavonic) epoch there will be – as was discussed earlier – a division of mankind into a good race and an evil one. And the evil race will look evil. The outer appearance of these people will reveal their inner nature. This means nothing other than that they will look more animal-like, that in them the human countenance will be distorted and will more resemble the physiognomy of animals. And this will happen because Michael is withdrawing from them. He will no longer bestow on all people, irrespective of their inner nature, the beauty and dignity of the human form. In the sixth epoch, which is no farther away in the future than the Roman Empire is in the past, the human form, the human countenance, will have to be earned; it will not simply be given. And this not very distant future has a foreshadowing which is even nearer to the present time.

In the lectures on the karma of the Anthroposophical Society we are told that the genuine anthroposophists will already in their next incarnation look different (Karmic Relationships, Vol.3, Aug 3, 1924). Irrespective of their racial or national background, their faces will have common features and these features will show the imprint of the spirit. And whose work will this be? From all we have considered in this context, it can only be Michael's.

One of the appellations of Michael used in the Old Testament and then again by Rudolf Steiner (especially in the Michaelmas prayer of the Christian Community) is the Countenance of God. It means that he reveals what is divine in the world and in man. He reveals it through the human form, through the human countenance. And he will in the future withhold this form from those who have no right to it.

All this is implied by the sixth seal, which shows Michael and the dragon. But this picture differs greatly from all traditional representations of Michael. There is no sword, no armour. Instead, Michael stands on the dragon and holds him with one hand on a chain whilst holding in the other hand a key. Michael's task as shown in this picture is not to destroy the dragon but to keep him 'under lock and key.' What are the chains, what is the key which can keep the Dragon down? It is intelligence. We are once again back to the theme which is as dominant in the Apocalypse as it is in Rudolf Steiner's Michael Letters.

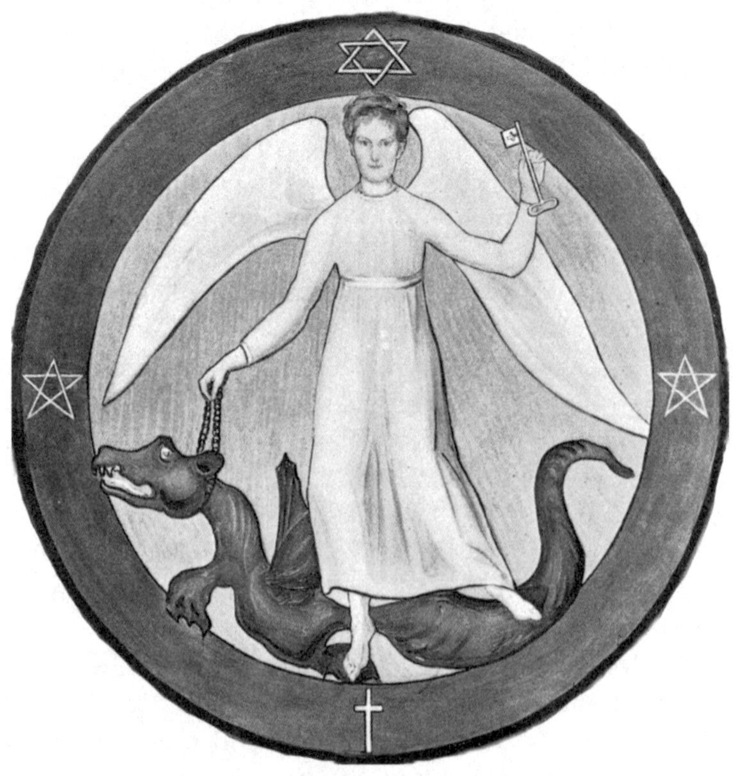

Sketch of the sixth seal of the Apocalypse

Once again we have to consider the moment in the evolution of mankind when individual intelligence became possible. In the middle of the Atlantean period the etheric forces of the head, which had been outside the physical head, were drawn in, and from then onwards coincided with it. The physical head is, however, a part of the whole human physical form and, as we have just discussed, this form was given by Michael. It was only when the etheric forces of the head were brought inside the Michael-given form that individual intelligence could awaken in man. Intelligence too has therefore to be regarded as owing to Michael.

The Greek myth tells of Pallas Athene, the goddess of intelligence, that she was not born of a mother but sprang fully grown and in full armour, with spear and shield, from the head of Zeus. One can see the resemblance between the armed goddess and the traditional image of the Archangel Michael. The being who arises from the forces of the head is Michaelic. And it was in Greece, in the centuries ruled by Michael, that intelligence reached the heights of the philosophies of Plato and Aristotle.

But just as the Atlantean period was the time when etheric forces had to be brought inside the physical head to make human intelligence possible, so the present age is the time when the faculty that man has developed by using his physical head – intelligence – should be freed from the head. This is Michael's aim in the present centuries of his rulership. The adversary powers want to bind intelligence even closer to the head, and we live in the midst of this battle. It is a battle with consequences that reach far into the future.

In as far as we are capable of freeing our thinking, our intelligence, from the physical head, we carry into the etheric body something that was not there before: the human tendency, the human form. When we study some anthroposophical text we are, of course, concerned with the particular subject; we study it to gain some information. But the real gain from a genuine, serious study is the development of new formative forces in the etheric body. One could say that the real gain is not information but 'formation' – the human formation of the etheric body which has, through its own nature, only animal tendencies. And in doing this we have made the first small step in the direction of the development of buddhi or life-spirit, in the direction indicated by the sixth seal. It will require far more than this to bring about the full 'humanisation' of the etheric body, but the first step, the freeing of intelligence from the physical head, has to be made in the present Michael Age.

To help humankind in this task a higher power than Michael has to come to our aid. There exists already a fully human etheric body, an etheric body without animal tendencies: the etheric Christ. His forces are present in the world to which our etheric body belongs and they can help us when our own strength is not sufficient. Michael and the etheric Christ work together at this time when man has to take a step forward in full freedom.

What is it that makes human intelligence so important that spiritual powers far above man fight about it? We use our intelligence to understand the world – which means the order in which things are related in space and time. Where there is chaos there is nothing to understand, but where there is a certain order, it needs intelligence to comprehend it. The Greek mystery schools and the writer of the Gospel of John called the power that creates order in the world the Logos which means the 'word.' From the orbits of the planets to the shape of a snowflake, from the growth of plants to the seven stages of cosmic evolution, from the laws of physics to the working of karma, it is all the manifestation of the Logos, of the word that was in the beginning. And our intelligence is the faculty which makes it possible that the logos can enter the human mind, the human soul. And this is what the Apocalypse describes: a rider on a white horse, and the name of that rider is The Word of God (Rev.19:13). He is the Lord of Lords and the King of Kings. The horse is again the symbol of intelligence and he who rides on it is Christ as the Logos.

But who will ride on the white steed depends on us. In a lecture Rudolf Steiner – using the symbol of a book instead of the horse – said, 'There is only one book, not two. And the only question is whether it is Christ or Ahriman who has the book. Yet Christ cannot have it unless mankind fights for it.

And this is the cosmic mission of spiritual science, the mission of the Michael stream.' (Influence of Lucifer and Ahriman, Nov 15, 1919). In this quotation the words 'cosmic mission' are used. It means a mission which goes beyond the present earth and is part of the cosmic evolution. And from what we have discussed we now know that this mission reaches into the future Venus stage, the stage symbolised by the image of Michael and the dragon in the sixth seal.

On the Venus stage human beings will have to transform the etheric body; the fight for human intelligence is already a fight for this transformation. If we regard the study of anthroposophy in this light, if we realise that this study calls for more than a mere reading, then we shall understand what Rudolf Steiner meant when he said, 'What I have spoken out of my physical body is only maya (illusion). Only what I speak out of my etheric body penetrates to the true reality.'

It is the 'etheric' speaking behind the physical which leads to Michael and to the intelligence symbolised by the key in his hand.

14

The New Jerusalem

Both the last chapters of the Apocalypse and Rudolf Steiner's seventh seal refer to the last, seventh, stage of evolution, the Vulcan stage, yet the two representations differ so much that one can hardly believe they deal with the same subject. The seventh seal shows a mysterious arrangement of symbols; the Apocalypse describes no less mysteriously a 'heavenly city,' the New Jerusalem. It will help us to come to some understanding of the two representations and their difference if we consider two aspects of this far-away future of man's evolution.

We know at present four stages of consciousness: the 'trance' consciousness, sleep, dream and waking consciousness. On the next planetary stage, Jupiter, we will have 'imagination' as our normal consciousness, on Venus 'inspiration' and on Vulcan 'intuition'. The white dove in the seventh seal, the symbol of the Holy Spirit, is here used as the symbol for the intuitive consciousness.

The other aspect of that future world of Vulcan arises from the relationship between the self and the other members of the human organism. On Jupiter the self will transform the astral body, on Venus the etheric body, on Vulcan the physical body. What the Apocalypse describes as the New Jerusalem is atma, the transformed physical body. The seventh seal can be seen as a symbol for 'intuition', the New Jerusalem as an image of atma. Yet the Apocalypse and the Seventh Seal have one feature in common: the cube. What is the meaning of the transparent cube in the seventh seal?

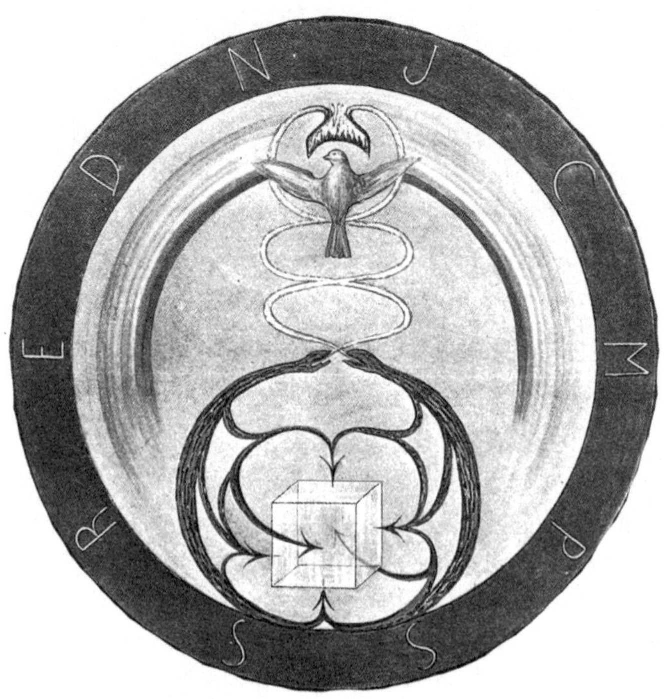

Sketch of the seventh seal of the Apocalypse

Rudolf Steiner explained that the three dimensions of space are, in the human organisation, not just neutral mathematical abstractions; each of them is a battlefield between Luciferic and Ahrimanic forces (*Balance in the World and Man*, Nov 21, 1914). Ahriman attacks us from the right-hand side, Lucifer from the left. Ahriman comes at us from behind, and Lucifer from in front of us. Ahriman works from below, and Lucifer from above.

But we are not completely exposed to these attacks. There is a region into which neither of them can penetrate. This region, protected by the gods, lies between the larynx and the diaphragm and between the breastbone and the spine. Rudolf Steiner calls this space in the middle part of our body a cube. The English designation 'chest' for this part conveys a similar idea.

This cube in our physical body is a sanctum, like the Holy of Holies in Solomon's Temple, which only the High Priest was allowed to enter. This sacred space within the Temple was an outward representation of that inner space from which Lucifer and Ahriman are barred. And this inner space between the larynx and diaphragm, between spine and breastbone, contains something which is very holy indeed. Rudolf Steiner spoke of it in the following verse:

> In the heart there lives a part of man
> Which contains, of all matter,
> That which is most spiritual
> And which, of all that lives spiritually,
> Manifests itself in the most material form.
> This is why the heart
> Is the sun in the microcosm of man
> And why man is, in his heart,
> At the deepest source of his being.

In the heart, spirit becomes matter and matter becomes spirit; this is the sun-mystery in the human organism and it is placed in the Holy of Holies, the cube, which Lucifer and Ahriman cannot enter.

What is the nature of this sun-power within man? The answer to this question has already been given in the Apocalypse, in the letter to the church of Ephesus. There Christ reproaches the members of that church who represent the Indian epoch, 'You have abandoned the love you had at first' (Rev.2:4). Human beings were drawn to earth, to their first incarnation, by love. After the Fall this love-force was divided, and so the two sexes came about. But something of that pure love-force that was in human beings at the beginning was saved. Protected from profanation it waits in the heart, within the cube, for the time in the distant future when people will be able to work with it consciously.

This is the secret of the transparent cube in the seventh seal.

It is a symbol of the future of Vulcan evolution when only this Holy of Holies will remain of the human being and when the forces which are now confined to the small space of the chest will become cosmic powers.

And what is the New Jerusalem of the Apocalypse? It is also described as a cube: length and breadth and height are equal. And it is also said that the heavenly city needs no sun, for God and the Lamb of God are the sun and the light of it. The Apocalypse speaks of this same cube that is shown in the seventh seal and the sun of the New Jerusalem is the heart – that part of man where he is at the deepest source of his being. The heart-forces are the centre of the Vulcan evolution. What will be their task?

Difficult as it is for us to form any idea of a future as far away as the Vulcan evolution, we can be certain that the seeds of even the most distant future are already present now; we have only to recognise them for what they are. In the lectures on The Karma of Vocation Rudolf Steiner speaks of such a seed of the Vulcan evolution.

He draws a comparison between a medieval artisan and a modern factory worker. The work done by a craftsman of the Middle Ages was such that human feeling could still flow into it. The personality of the worker could still find expression in the work. This is not possible for the factory-hand of the present, for a man working on the assembly line. There cannot be any connection between his personality and his work. You may regard this aspect of the machine age as regrettable, but Rudolf Steiner uses in this lecture a strange word to describe the soul's attitude towards such work. He calls it 'chaste'. Precisely because the soul remains untouched by the work, precisely because there is no personal satisfaction in performing the work, it is 'chaste'. Seen in this context the work of an actor on the stage or of a musician is not 'chaste' because they enjoy what they are doing. And – so it is said in the lecture of November 12, 1916 – through this 'chaste' element in the human soul engaged in the mechanical and monotonous factory work, there arise forces for the final stage of evolution, for Vulcan. It is the personality of the worker which is excluded from factory work; he is by force of circumstance made to disregard his own personality in his work. And the Vulcan evolution is the stage on which 'personality' comes to an end.

Spiritual science makes a clear distinction between 'personality' and 'individuality'. We are in each of our incarnations a different personality yet remain always the same individuality. After death we gradually shed the personality of the past incarnation and return to our immortal individuality. Perhaps an analogy taken from musical life can make the distinction clear.

A man sings as a member of a choir. His voice makes an individual and necessary contribution to the performances of the choir. He would, however, have no means of expressing his personality in his singing unless he had to sing a solo part at the concert. The individuality plays a unique and specific part in the larger context of the choir. The personality comes to expression in the solo part. Taking the analogy still further, we realise that there are occasions when each member of the choir is compelled to sing solo: when they practise their part for a particular concert. The purpose of the practice is to be able to sing one's part in the choir as well as possible. And this is a perfect analogy to the purpose of the soul's incarnation: we live as a certain personality in order to develop and perfect the part we have to sing in the great choir of mankind.

The immortal individuality (or the higher self or ego as we usually call it) knows itself as an integral part of mankind. The transient, mortal personality may believe in its own importance but, in reality, it only has value in as far as it gathers experiences and develops faculties which are of benefit to the self, the individuality, and this means for mankind as a whole.

The personality is bound up with the existence in a physical body. It began on Ancient Saturn with the first physical bodies, which then consisted only of warmth. The beings who incarnated in these bodies are the Archai or Spirits of Time, but Rudolf Steiner also calls them Spirits of Personality.

On Vulcan, the last stage of evolution, the physical body is to be transformed to become atma – the human spirit-form. And with this spiritualisation of the physical body there comes also the end of the experience, 'I am this or that personality', What remains is the individuality. It was said before that the individuality can be compared with a voice singing in a choir. But this is also the essence of the description of the Vulcan stage given by Rudolf Steiner in his lecture of December 9, 1923 (Mystery Knowledge). On Vulcan everything is living speech. Word resounds to word, word reveals itself to word, word speaks to word. And man feels himself as the word which understands the world.

This is what 'individuality' means: to know oneself as a word within the cosmic Word, the Logos who was in the beginning but who also will be at the end, for he is the Alpha and the Omega. And this is also what the Apocalypse wants to convey by the image of the New Jerusalem.

The choice of the name Jerusalem for that world of the future, Vulcan, has a profound reason. As was mentioned before, on Vulcan the physical body will be transformed to spirit-man or atma. But such a transformed physical body appeared here on earth with the resurrection of Christ. And such was the power of this event that it changed the spiritual aura of the region where it had occurred. In a lecture given on Rudolf Steiner described how the souls of the dead see the earth (The Earth Seen by the Dead, April 1, 1918). In the east, towards Asia, the aura of the earth shows a blue-violet glow. In the west, in America, fiery yellow-red colours predominate. In between, in the European region, there is a band of green. But there is one place on earth where the aura differs from this general rainbow scheme. In this place can be seen a golden form, like golden crystals which are, however, life filled. And the whole impression is that of a golden star shining from this place which is the city of Jerusalem.

Rudolf Steiner adds to this description that this view of the Holy City from the spiritual world was the reason why the author of the Apocalypse called the final stage of man's evolution the New Jerusalem. In the world of imagination colours are not accidental. They say something. What is the golden star in the aura of Jerusalem saying?

In the memoirs of an old member there is a story about a meeting of Theosophists in Paris where Rudolf Steiner was present. Someone mentioned the Great Sphinx of Giza, the huge stone figure with the human head and the lion's body which lies, like a guardian, in front of the Pyramids. The question arose as to why the face of this sphinx is smiling. Rudolf Steiner answered, 'The sphinx looks into a far-distant future when all the errors and all the wrongs, and when all the sorrows and all the pains are forgotten, and mankind has arrived at its goal. That is why the sphinx is smiling.'

And almost the same words appear in the Apocalypse describing the New Jerusalem:

> '[God] will wipe away every tear from their eyes, and death shall be no more, neither shall there be mourning nor crying nor pain any more, for the former things have passed away.'
>
> And he that sat upon the throne said, 'Behold, I make all things new.' (Rev.21:4f)

This is what the golden light over Jerusalem promises: harmony and peace. And the name of the Holy City contains the same promise because Jerusalem means the holy dwelling of peace.

The two themes wisdom and love (or intelligence and love) underlie the whole interpretation of the Apocalypse by Rudolf Steiner. In the opening lecture the two themes are introduced by references to Hegel and Caspar Hauser. They are then proclaimed in a different form by the being who speaks 'I am the Alpha and the Omega.' They are then shown to us as the two pillars Jachim and Boaz. And whilst the fifth seal, the woman standing on the moon, speaks of the transformation of love, the sixth seal, Michael and the dragon, indicates the transformation of intelligence. The seventh stage brings the culmination where wisdom and love become one in the 'holy dwelling of peace', Jerusalem. The evolution of mankind is a story with a 'happy ending', divine peace. That is why the Sphinx is smiling.

Bibliography

Steiner, Rudolf. Volume Nos refer to the Collected Works (CW), or to the German Gesamtausgabe (GA).

—, Anthroposophical Leading Thoughts (CW 26) Rudolf Steiner Press, UK 1998.

—, Balance in the World and Man, (part of CW 158) Steiner Book Centre, Canada 1977.

—, Christianity as Mystical Fact (CW 8) Anthroposophic Press, USA 1997.

—, Cosmic and Human Metamorphoses (CW 175)

—, Curative Education Course, see Education for Special Needs.

—, 'The Earth Seen by the Dead,' The Golden Blade 1986 (part of CW 181).

—, Education as a Force for Social Change (CW 296) Anthroposophic Press, USA 1997.

—, Education for Special Needs, the Curative Education Course (CW 317) Rudolf Steiner Press, UK 1998.

—, Esoteric Lessons (CW 266) SteinerBooks, USA 2011.

—, Esoteric Science (CW 13) Anthroposophic Press, USA 1998.

—, The Foundations of Human Existence (CW 293) Anthroposophic Press, USA 1996, also published as The Study of Man.

—, The Influence of Lucifer and Ahriman (part of CW 191) Anthroposophic Press, USA 1993.

—, Inner Impulses of Evolution (part of CW 171) Anthroposophic Press, USA 1984.

—, The Karma of Vocation (CW 172) Anthroposophic Press, USA 1984.

—, Karmic Relationships, Vol.3, CW 237) Rudolf Steiner Press, UK 2009.

—, Knowledge of Higher Worlds (CW 10) Rudolf Steiner Press, UK 2004.

—, Man as Symphony of the Creative Word (CW 230) Rudolf Steiner Press, UK 1991.

—, Michael Letters, see Anthroposophical Leading Thoughts.

—, Mystery Knowledge and Mystery Centres (CW 232) Rudolf Steiner Press, UK 2013.

—, Nine Lectures on Bees, (CW 351) St George Books, USA 1971.

—, Rosicrucianism Renewed (CW 284) SteinerBooks, USA 2007.

—, Spiritual Science as a Foundation for Social Forms (CW 199) Anthroposophic Press, USA 1986.

—, The Study of Man (CW 293) Rudolf Steiner Press, UK 2004, also published as The Foundations of Human Existence.

—, Supersensible Man (CW 231) Anthroposophical Publishing Co, London 1961.

—, Theosophy (CW 9) Anthroposophic Press, USA 1994.

—, Towards Imagination, (CW 169) Anthroposophic Press, USA 1990.

The Spiritual Background to Christian Festivals

Charles Kovacs

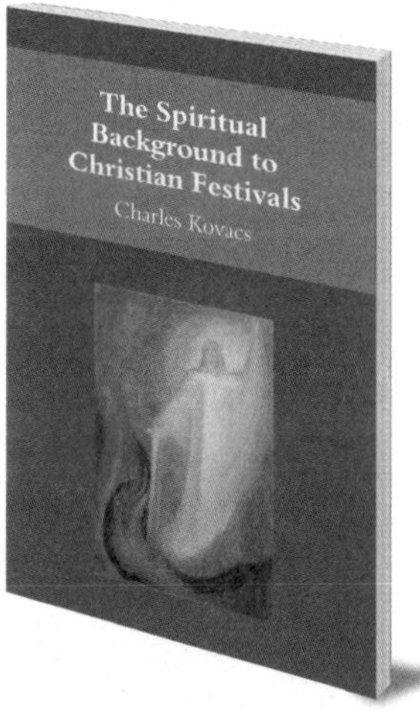

The rhythms of the earth can be seen in, for example, the daily cycle of day and night, or in the changing seasons. Rudolf Steiner spoke about how Christian festivals such as Easter, Whitsun and Christmas fitted not just into these patterns, but also into larger cosmic rhythms and, on a smaller scale, human rhythms.

In this concise book Charles Kovacs explores the structure of our calendar year and looks in detail at the background to each Christian festival.

florisbooks.co.uk

Christianity and the Ancient Mysteries

Reflections on Rudolf Steiner's Christianity as Mystical Fact

Charles Kovacs

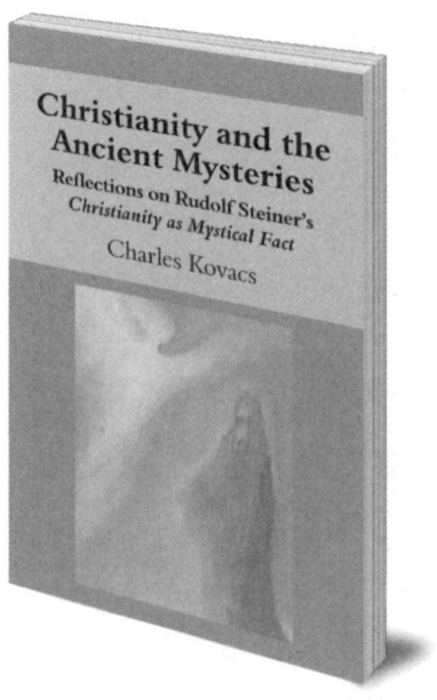

Charles Kovacs brings his deep knowledge of esoteric writings, mythology and Steiner's lectures to show how the way for Christianity was prepared in the ancient pre-Christian mysteries of Egypt and Greece. He discusses the symbolic and real events of the gospels, as well as looking at some of the understandings and disputes of the early Christians.

florisbooks.co.uk

Waldorf education books by Charles Kovacs

Class 4 (age 9–10)
Norse Mythology

Classes 4 and 5 (age 9–11)
The Human Being and the Animal World

Classes 5 and 6 (age 10–12)
Ancient Greece
Botany

Class 6 (age 11–12)
Ancient Rome

Classes 6 and 7 (age 11–13)
Geology and Astronomy

Class 7 (age 12–13)
The Age of Discovery

Classes 7 and 8 (age 12–14)
Muscles and Bones

Class 8 (age 13–14)
The Age of Revolution

Class 11 (age 16–17)
Parsifal and the Search for the Grail

florisbooks.co.uk

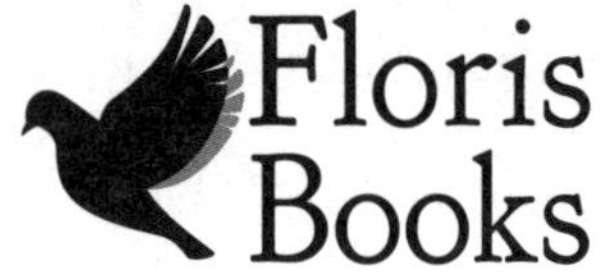

For news on all our **latest books,**
and to receive **exclusive discounts,**
join our mailing list at:

florisbooks.co.uk

Plus subscribers get a FREE book
with every online order!

We will never pass your details to anyone else.